Practicing

the Presence

of God

for Practical Purposes

Practicing the Presence of God for Practical Purposes

by

**Deborah G. Whitehouse
and
C. Alan Anderson**

Copyright © 2000 by Deborah Whitehouse and Alan Anderson
All rights reserved.
No part of this book may be reproduced without written permission from the publisher, except by a reviewer who may quote brief passages or reproduce illustrations in a review; nor may any part of this book be reproduced, stored in a retrieval system, or transmitted in any form or by any means electronic, mechanical, photocopying, recording, or other, without written permission from the authors.

This book is manufactured in the United States of America.

ISBN: 1-58820-264-X

This book is printed on acid free paper.

1stBooks - rev. 10/30/00

Contents

Preface vii

1. Our Story Begins 1
    Science and Insanity 3
    Where Covey Got the Seven Habits 6
    Ancient Roots 11
    Health 14
    Wealth 15
    Happiness 15
    Putting It Together 16
    The Philosophy to be Tested 19
    Our Purpose 23

2. Practicing 27
    What Practice Involves 29
    How to Get to Carnegie Hall 38
    But How Do I Do It? 42
    An Adult Partnership 44
    Getting In the Habit 46
    All We Like Sheep Have Gone Astray 47
    Changing Beliefs 50
    Practice as the Path 53
    Summary 58

3. The Presence of God 61
    Metaphysical Metamorphosis 64
    Which Breed of God Should I Pick? 70
    Jesus 76
    The Arrival of the Cavalry, German Style 82
    God: Up Close and Personal 85
    God's Mind and God's Body 86
    Changing the Pattern of the Past 87
    Hell, and Other Graceless States 89
    Open at the Top 91
    Study vs. Treatment 92

  Portrait— er, Movie of God, New Every Moment 94
  What About God's Body? 95

4. Practical Purposes 99
  Affirmative Prayer 102
  Health 107
  Wealth 116
  Happiness 126
  Relationships 130
  Divine Guidance 131

5. The Black Hole 135
  Evil 135
  Did Brother Lawrence Have Bad Hair Days? 141
  Sin, Original and Unoriginal, Which It Mostly Is 143
  What To Do When the Roof Falls In 145
  Grief 146
  Illness 146
  Financial Challenges 147
  Relationship Difficulties 149
  Feelings, Who-o-oa Feelings 151
  Toxicity and Cults 152
  Grownup or Adult? 153
  In Parting 158

Bibliography 161

Preface

This book is in the tradition of a more-than-century-old something called New Thought. At the turn of the century, William James referred to it as "mind-cure" and "the religion of healthy-mindedness." Much of the theory of New Thought has remained largely unchanged decade after decade, crumbling or revealing gaps bit by bit in comparison with newer, more adequate thought unavailable to the founders of the movement. This book is part of a new wave in New Thought, reconsidering and to a considerable extent replacing its unsound underpinnings—providing a new conceptual foundation for a beautiful house in which many have lived happily and healthily. That house is big enough for you to move in, or, if you prefer, just to gain some inspiration and help from visiting for a while.

This book is for people who think that they ought to be getting more out of life and aren't sure of how to go about doing it—or who think that they do know how but are finding that it isn't working well.

This book is for people who are doing a great job of working with God, yet would like to have a better understanding of what they are doing.

This book is for people who believe in God, and for those who don't but are willing to think about it.

This book is about using God in your life. Lest "using God" seem irreligious or sneaky, we hasten to add that we believe that it is impossible not to use God. This is because God is so intimately involved with us that apart from God, we could not be at all.

This book is for people who are willing to consider that our lives are responses to offers made to us by God. We are concerned with using God better by more consistently saying yes to these divine offers.

This book does not say that God is all there is (as many of our friends believe). It is a book for people who are open to considering that God is real, here, everywhere, and indispensable without being everything. We see pantheism (the belief that God is all) as an early aberration within New Thought, departing from the essential insights of Phineas Parkhurst Quimby, who is generally recognized as the father of New Thought. It may have seemed reasonable at one time, but its usefulness is ended as one comes to recognize the pan*en*theistic (all is *in* God) position of a process perspective.

God has one job and we have another, and not much gets done constructively in our lives if we don't (knowingly or unknowingly) work with God, rather than against God's loving, guiding wisdom. God never fails to do God's part in our lives, but we often fail to do ours. All creation is co-creation between God and someone or something else; that is a major theme of the book.

This is not a New Age book, at least in any narrow, conventional meaning of that term. It's a book written in a new age and supporting a particular vision for the new age, but it is not New Age in the sense associated with an amorphous movement revolving around pantheism, crystals, channeling, astrology, and almost anything else that used to seem strange but now is popular in many quarters.

As the title indicates, this is a book about the practice of the presence of God for practical purposes. We'll take up one by one the ideas contained in the title, and we'll show how they work together to bring us health, wealth, and happiness.

If you're interested, read on.

1. Our Story Begins

Once upon a time, in seventeenth-century France, to be exact, there lived a monk who was so happy, so good-humored, and so obviously close to God that he became known far beyond the walls of his monastery, and his spiritual advice was sought by great and small alike. The monk was known as Brother Lawrence of the Resurrection, and the secret of his happy spirituality he freely shared with all. He called it "the practice of the Presence of God."

Brother Lawrence did not start out as what we would call a mystic, a person who experiences God directly, intuitively. After a checkered career in the military, during which he was captured by the enemy on one occasion and wounded on another, he took a position as a footman to a great lord. However, as he described himself, he was "a clumsy lummox who broke everything," and so, haunted by memories of the horrors of war and seemingly unfit for anything else, he decided to "give myself entirely to God in reparation for my sins, and to renounce everything for His love." He became a Carmelite friar, and for the first ten years he was as miserable as before, assigned to menial tasks in the kitchen. Although he meditated during his prayer time on death, judgment, hell, paradise, and his sins; the rest of the time, even during his work, he devoted himself to "the presence of God whom I felt was always near me, often in the deepest recesses of my heart, a practice which so heightened my concept of God that only faith was capable of satisfying me about this concept." Gradually this practice spread even to his prayer time, to his "great delight and great consolation." "I suddenly found myself changed," he wrote, "and my soul, which up till then was always disturbed, experienced a profound interior peace as if it had found its center and a place of peace." His translator explains,

> For Lawrence, the ultimate goal of every soul is union with God. Though he knew the perfect union can

take place only after death, he believed we can achieve a far greater degree of unity with God in this life than most people think is possible. The way to accomplish this is through practicing the presence of God.

Two things are required: to abandon oneself completely to God, completely trusting in God's goodness and mercy; and simultaneously, carrying on a continual conversation with God, enabling us to invoke God's presence with us all the time. Brother Lawrence adds, "All these acts of adoration should be made by faith." He explains that at first it takes persistent effort to form the habit of continually talking with God, but it eventually becomes easier. He cautions against getting bogged down in particular practices and neglecting love. Despite what was obviously a poor self-image, he eventually came to see himself as utterly loved and aided by God in everything he did all day long, with any mistakes he made forgiven. He eventually developed proficiency in his chores, with God's help.

Others were able to see past Brother Lawrence's gruff exterior to the love of God shining through him, and he advises, "Always see God and His glory in everything we do, say, and undertake," so he evidently saw God in others, as well. He claimed that he felt more united to God during ordinary activities than during religious activities, which left him with what his translator refers to as "a profound spiritual dryness." He sums things up with characteristic simplicity:

> We cannot avoid the dangers and perils with which life abounds without the actual and unceasing help of God; let us ask His help continually. How can we ask for His help unless we are with Him? How can we be with Him except by thinking of Him often? How can we think of Him often except by forming a holy habit of

doing so? . . . I do not know of an easier or more appropriate method.

The scene now shifts to the end of the twentieth century, to a much more complex world. Despite all its advances in science and medicine, people are just as soul-sick as Brother Lawrence was before he hit on his practice. Our understanding of our minds and bodies has evolved, however, as has our understanding of spirituality. We now see that our spirituality includes our minds, bodies, and emotions, and we have a better grasp of the relationship between mind and body and of the way the mind works. With the same dedication that Brother Lawrence showed in his monastery, we can take his practice out into the world and apply it to our lives with an impact he could never have dreamed of. We can use the practice of the presence of God not only for peace of mind in a contemplative state, but for practical purposes as well. We can use it to heal bodies, minds, and pocketbooks, to prosper ourselves and others in all possible ways. We can learn how to work with God as our wise and loving partner in all that we do, just as Brother Lawrence did, but with a worldview far more advanced than his. Standing on his shoulders, we can see farther.

Science and Insanity

In the history of ideas, we denizens of planet Earth have reached what for lack of a better name is known as the postmodern era. At the moment, it consists of a peculiar sort of crossroads: the possibility of despairing, godless, unprincipled nihilism in which everything is relative and there is no star to steer by; or the possibility of newly evolved spirituality of a higher order in which everything is related, a spirituality that embraces and uplifts the great advances of science. We have come to this lady-or-tiger scenario as a result of modern-era efforts to break free from medieval superstition and limited thinking. These efforts may have succeeded so well that they threaten to destroy the very thing they were trying to rescue: the human psyche. Here's why:

Mystics and other wise people describe three ways of gathering knowledge, three eyes, as the mystics put it. The first is the eye of flesh, empirical knowing. This is the eye of science, the eye that deals with the material world of the physical senses. The second eye is the eye of reason, the mental eye. This is the eye of philosophy, the eye of the intellect, which uses critical thinking and analysis dispassionate from the fray. The third eye is the eye of contemplation, which deals with mystical knowing. The eye of reason is supposed to mediate between the other two eyes in order to keep all three eyes in balance.

Problems in knowing arise when one eye usurps the roles of the other two. One famous example was the medieval scholars' attempt to determine the number of teeth in a horse's mouth by deduction (the eye of mind) instead of by going out to the stable and counting them (the eye of flesh). Nearly every major religion has suffered from that type of error: being expert in contemplation does not automatically make one expert in the realms of the other two eyes. As Ken Wilber puts it in his book, *Eye to Eye*, "anytime one eye tries to see for another eye, blurred vision results." He continues,

> Buddhism and Christianity and other genuine religions contained, at their summit, ultimate insights into ultimate reality, but these transverbal insights were invariably all mixed up with rational truths and empirical facts. Humanity had not, as it were, yet learned to differentiate and separate the eyes of flesh, reason, and contemplation. . . . the philosophers came in and destroyed the rational side of religion, and science came in and destroyed the empirical side. However, theology.

Our Story Begins

. . was so heavily dependent upon its rationalism and its empirical "facts" (the sun circles the earth as the Bible says), that when these two eyes were taken away by philosophy and science, Western spirituality all but went blind. It did not fall back on its eye of contemplation—but merely fell apart and spent its time in futile argument with the philosophers and scientists. From that point on, spirituality in the West was dismantled, and only philosophy and science seriously remained.

Within a century, however, philosophy as a rational system—a system based on the eye of mind—was in its own turn decimated, and decimated by the new scientific empiricism. At that point, human knowledge was *reduced* to only the eye of flesh.

In addition to the problems of destructive postmodernism and the closing of two of our three eyes, we face the problem of toxic faith. Brother Lawrence somehow managed to triumph over this problem with even less understanding available to him than is available to us. Too many religions still teach children that they are rotten sinners, no good, doomed to everlasting hell and damnation unless they do what their leaders tell them to do; and even then, one cannot be sure of "salvation." The damage that this does to self-esteem lasts far into adulthood, and is sometimes never healed. Psychology now teaches us about the self-fulfilling prophecy: that if we tell people they are no good, they will live up to their reputation!

One problem that Brother Lawrence did not have to face was the separation of church and state. In the United States today, the original intent to ensure freedom *of* religion has largely been replaced by governmentally enforced freedom *from* religion. Public schools have been frightened out of teaching ethical standards and facts about religion, so an entire generation or more of children has grown up without knowledge of the Ten

Commandments or other moral codes based on universal principles that forbid stealing, lying, or harming people and property. Absence of religious influence has led to absence of kindness, politeness, and service to others. Emphasis on having a pleasing personality so one can "get ahead" has eclipsed emphasis on an underlying foundation of good character, with such qualities as integrity, courage, and perseverance.

Business consultant Stephen Covey has provided us with a simple method for dealing with the loss of the character ethic: put it back. In a series of books beginning with the best-selling *Seven Habits of Highly Effective People*, he emphasizes the importance of leading principle-centered lives. Principles, he maintains, are guidelines for successful living that are to be found in all the major religions and in every culture throughout history. We need to center our lives on such principles, and live by them. To center on anything else: work, family, spouse, church, possessions, or even self, is to risk losing the very thing centered on. Only these time-tested principles, external to ourselves, are adequate to build a life around, to serve as a North Star to steer by. Covey believes that these principles come from the ultimate source, which most of us refer to as God.

Where Covey Got the Seven Habits

Covey developed his ingenious model of the Seven Habits and the principles on which they rest from his study of two hundred years of American success literature. (A similar study was undertaken at approximately the same time by journalist Richard Huber.) From the last third of the nineteenth century to the present, that literature springs from or is heavily influenced by New Thought, a philosophico-religious movement originating in New England with a self-educated clockmaker named Phineas Parkhurst Quimby, who believed he had rediscovered the lost healing methods of Jesus. What he had discovered was the

Our Story Begins

power of the God-aligned mind to heal and prosper. Other New Thought founders soon introduced themes from Eastern religions, and New Thought continues to serve as a link between East and West.

Practical spirituality is the awareness of God at work in our everyday lives. New Thought involves a definite set of practices that are built on, center on, and revolve around our concept of God. It begins with changing our thought and using our willpower to sustain the change and follow through with action. It won't happen without 1) faith in a God and a universe that support and justify this, 2) a clear picture of what we want, and 3) practical skills for follow-through. Mind-power alone is not readily sustained; if the changed consciousness is not God-centered, it will fall apart in the low times that we all experience. And faith in a God that is other than unconditionally loving or in a universe of lack and limitation isn't going to work. The great philosopher Alfred North Whitehead found that in developing a model of what the universe must be like in order to be at all, he could find no explanation for the novelty in the world without the presence of God. We would be stuck in the same old ruts of failure and poverty and illness, were it not for the loving God at work in the world. And why would anyone bother to adhere to a system of values during tough times without some assurance that God is there in the midst of things, loving and luring us on to greater good, suffering as we suffer, rejoicing as we rejoice? It would be all too tempting to succumb to expediency, or just to give up in despair. As Episcopal priest and New Thoughter Leo Booth likes to put it, "Show me what kind of person you are and I'll show you what God you believe in."

New Thought teaches that we are spiritual beings having a human experience in a good and abundant universe, that we are all inescapably involved with a loving God, and that by changing one's thinking one can change any condition in one's life. It is positive, optimistic, and upbeat. It is simple, but not always easy, for it demands the development of strong character. It is a way of life, which must include one's philosophy and one's system of beliefs, attitudes, and actions, which combination is the best definition of religion. But you shouldn't merely swallow someone else's answers to the great philosophical questions without thinking them through for yourself, so New Thought is also pragmatic, which is philosopherese for "go check it out yourself and see whether it works for you."

Medical experts now state that more than ninety percent of all illnesses are mental in origin, and most of the other ills that beset the human race are equally mental in their basis, for the universe is mental in nature, more like a great thought than a great machine, as the great scientist Sir James Jeans observed.

Recent research in medicine and psychology has shown that positive thoughts can have a positive effect on body chemistry and that optimists do better than pessimists on just about any measure you care to name. New Thought is systematically applied optimism. It is the rigorous mental discipline of keeping one's thoughts off of what one does not want and on what one does want, as long as what one wants is consistent with the natural and moral laws of the universe. It is largely based on the teachings of Jesus, and hence, God-centered. As New Thoughter Marianne Williamson writes,

> I had heard it said that God was love, but it had never kicked in for me exactly what that meant. . . . He is the love within us. Whether we "follow Him," i.e., think with love, is entirely up to us. When we choose to love, or to allow our minds to be one with God, then life is wonderful. When we turn away from love, the pain sets in. So when we think with God, then life is peaceful.

Our Story Begins

When we think without Him, life is painful. And that's the mental choice we make, every moment of every day.

Earl Nightingale, the late great radio personality, once made a record that sold over a million copies, quite a feat at the time. Its title was "The Strangest Secret," and it changed lives. The secret is, "We become what we think about all day long," and what is strange about it is that it is a secret. The New Thought movement is dedicated to teaching people how to govern what they think about, how to achieve their own health, wealth, and happiness in a way that helps everybody else in the process. This involves cocreation with the source of all the newness in the world, commonly known as God.

When our first jointly written book, *New Thought: A Practical American Spirituality*, appeared, many New Thoughters pounced on it with cries of glee. They welcomed it as an opportunity to fill in gaps in their knowledge and explore new ideas that built on ideas with which they were already familiar.

However, people unfamiliar with New Thought tended to react differently. Some cast suspicious sideways glances at the book on display, making comments such as "What's New Thought?" or "I was just getting used to Old Thought!" If it was new, why hadn't they read about it in *The New York Times* or seen it on *Good Morning America*, since it's American? And spirituality, isn't that something like religion, which we all know has nothing to do with *thinking*; heck, most churches would prefer that we didn't think too much. Doesn't sound very practical. Besides, the rent is due; no time for reading books unless they pertain to that rotten job or shaping up those no-good kids or getting along better with the spouse or "sig." And did somebody say that the book was about theology or philosophy or something? God, not that!

Chapter One

All right, we agree that as the name of a spiritual movement, *New Thought* leaves a lot to be desired. So did its predecessors: *Mind Cure*, *Mental Science*, and *The Boston Craze*. So do its descendants, *Positive Thinking* and *Possibility Thinking*. Even brand names such as *Unity* or *Religious Science* don't really tell the whole story. So, here goes again: We're talking about the universal longing for health, wealth, and happiness. And we're saying—the entire New Thought movement is saying—that the way to acquire health, wealth, and happiness is through the practice of the presence of God for practical purposes.

Sooner or later, everyone notices that the world is not precisely as he or she would like it to be. People react to this observation in myriad ways, one of the most popular being screaming, which is not popular with other people in the vicinity, so screamers branch out into other more socially acceptable behaviors. The most useful of these, though not, alas! the most frequently chosen, is to become philosophical.

Philosophy, as Alan describes it, is an armchair activity. One sits aloof from the fray and ponders such questions as What kind of world is this? What is worth having? What should I really want? and How can I get what I really want in this kind of world? Having used the thinking-and-logic half of one's brain to come up with answers to these questions, one then decides how one ought to behave, based on those answers. One's success in getting what one wants is determined by how well one follows through on one's decisions. This is a function of one's *character*, about which we will have a lot more to say later on.

The fly in the ointment is that all too often the fledgling philosopher fails to use his/her brain power, and substitutes someone else's answers. And just like copying answers off someone else's paper in a math exam, someone else's answers may be wrong. You can't cheat on your meaning-of-life exam, or you won't get satisfactory results.

One characteristic of Americans—at least, the ones you run into in the United States—is that they tend to pick and choose what they like, cafeteria style, when presented with a system of beliefs. This is getting off to a good start, and it's the main reason that New Thought originated in America rather than somewhere else. However, many, if not most, Americans fail to follow through. They don't make sure that their selections are compatible with one another, and the absence of compatibility can lead to metaphysical indigestion. Also, many Americans don't develop sufficient strength of character to follow through on the behaviors that need to flow from their beliefs if they are to get what they want.

New Thought does not require allegiance to any particular set of beliefs, though it has some commonalities found throughout its various branches. It is very much a do-it-yourself religion, and as a result, many of its practitioners deny that they are New Thoughters, because they have put together their own blend of beliefs. This is particularly true of the major brands of New Thought: Divine Science, Unity, and Religious Science, each of which has its own characteristic slant; for example, Unity School of Christianity refers to what it teaches as "Practical Christianity." Their commonalities are vastly more numerous and important than their differences. Still, one of the nice things about New Thought is that it accommodates individual preferences.

Ancient Roots

Although New Thought does incorporate some nineteenth- and twentieth-century thought of great importance, it is often said that there is nothing new in New Thought, because it springs from ancient roots. However, what's most practically or significantly new in New Thought is *your* thought. New Thought is quintessentially American in that it breaks away from religious tyranny, the tyranny of toxic religious beliefs. New Thought teachings are mostly based on the Bible, although it accepts teachings from other sources as well. New Thought teaches that Jesus more than any other human being understood and made use of his own indwelling divinity, which he referred to as "the Father . . . in me" (John 10:38, 14:10, 11). New Thoughters do not worship Jesus because it wouldn't make sense and because Jesus did not ask to be worshipped. Rather, he taught his followers to love one another and to keep his commandments, which mainly dealt with the law of mind action (As in mind, so in manifestation; as in heaven, so on earth). We have dealt at greater length with believing Jesus as opposed to believing *in* Jesus in our first book. This is much of what sets New Thought apart from traditional Christianity. But New Thought does not demand adherence to a particular creed, and it is perfectly possible to accept general New Thought principles and still be a loyal parishioner at your local church or synagogue. If, on the other hand, you are unchurched and would like to be churched, check a World Wide Web search engine for "New Thought movement," or the New Thought movement home page (websyte.com/alan), for links to lists of New Thought churches, both brand-name and independent.

America was settled by people who sought to worship God in the way they saw fit, and New Thought carries this even farther by encouraging each person to develop an individual tailor-made religion. Certainly, if we're smart, we'll check our own ideas and understandings against those of other people who seem to have their acts together. The Methodists do a good job of this with their quadrilateral consisting of Scripture, tradition, reason, and experience as mutually corrective. Put them all together, they spell balance, which increases the likelihood that they are a close approximation of truth. New Thought has also been influenced by ancient Eastern wisdom from Taoism, Hinduism, and Buddhism. Its most significant non-ancient literary root is probably the writings of Ralph Waldo Emerson, who was in turn influenced by Eastern thought.

New Thought looks to Jesus as Way-Shower (to borrow Emerson's term), whatever an individual's beliefs about him may be. Jesus had the mind of Christ and made the most of it; we seek to emulate him, for we, too, have "the mind of Christ," as St. Paul told us (1 Cor. 2:16), the spark of the divine. Jesus quoted Psalm 82:6, "Ye are gods." He told his disciples that they would be able to do greater works than those they saw him do (John 14:12), and the Bible records that the disciples did indeed work miracles. As later generations of Christians slid off into superstitious thinking and abdicated their own responsibility in the face of what they believed to be their depraved and sinful nature, they disempowered themselves. They failed to use their miracle-working ability, and so, miracles became rare.

Marianne Williamson, in *A Return to Love*, in a passage frequently misattributed to Nelson Mandela, states:

> Our deepest fear is not that we are inadequate. Our deepest fear is that we are powerful beyond measure. It is our light, not our darkness, that most frightens us. We ask ourselves, Who am I to be brilliant, gorgeous, talented, fabulous? Actually, who are you *not* to be? You are a child of God. Your playing small doesn't serve the world. There's nothing enlightened about shrinking so that other people won't feel insecure around you. We are all meant to shine, as children do. We were born to make manifest the glory of God that is within us. It's not just in some of us; it's in everyone. And as we let our own light shine, we unconsciously give other

people permission to do the same. As we're liberated from our own fear, our presence automatically liberates others. (p. 165)

The rise of science, seeking to combat superstition, and the dominance of materialism contributed to the absence of miracles. But the universe is still God's body, still abundant, still awaiting our recognition of our miracle-working powers, for a miracle is not a suspension of natural law, but rather, can be defined as the operation of a law that we do not yet fully understand. As Whitehead puts it, God is "the chief exemplification" of "all metaphysical principles" rather than the great exception. God, being utterly reliable, cannot violate natural laws, which in one way or another have arisen through God's guidance, and there's a lot that we don't yet understand, so there's plenty of room for miracles in an orderly, lawful universe. New Thought is not about the supernatural; instead, it holds a view of God as both immanent in nature and transcending it. The laws of mind operate just as dependably as the law of gravity. Quimby and the other New Thought founders talked of science, using the term differently than we do today to refer to standardized methods used to gather information for the prediction and control of natural events. To them, science referred directly or indirectly to God, in opposition to superstition or the supernatural, which they were doing their best to avoid.

Health

Quimby's healing methods involved his mind's working on the patient's mind, disputing the erroneous beliefs of the patient, for Quimby believed that "the explanation is the cure." Just as their beliefs, their faith in illness, had made them sick, their faith, as Jesus said (Matt. 9:21) had made them whole again. Today, New Thought still seeks to heal by the power of mind—human mind, in conjunction with divine mind—by prayer, but also makes use of both orthodox and alternative medicine.

Wealth

It didn't take long for people who had been healed by the power of mind to realize that the same power could heal their pocketbooks and spirits as well. Traditional Christianity often paints Jesus as poor; a careful reading of the New Testament reveals a very different picture. The stories tell how Jesus as an infant received rich gifts from the Magi. As an adult, he wore a rare and expensive seamless garment, dined with the wealthy, and paid his taxes with a coin found in the mouth of a fish. When he died, his body was buried in a rich man's tomb. Clearly, he saw himself as the rich child of a loving heavenly father, like the father in his parable of the Prodigal Son; and he told us in the words of the father in the parable, "all that I have is thine" (Luke 15:31).

Jesus also taught abundance, and New Thought recognizes that God is fully present and available everywhere, so as the rich children of a loving, heavenly parent, all of us can expect to prosper. Jesus explained that we must ask for what we want with the expectancy that we are receiving it, and that we must also give in order to receive, so that the good is kept in circulation. He told us, "Give, and it shall be given unto you, good measure, pressed down, and shaken together and running over" (Luke 6:38).

Happiness

Happiness is a state of enhanced satisfaction, enhanced by intensifying our attention on whatever we find satisfactory. Research has shown this to be a left-hemisphere function. In other words, happiness depends upon our thinking. Once again, the power of the mind can bring us whatever we desire. It can help us to have better relationships and to find greater pleasure in our life's work. Later in this book we will examine ways to go about this.

Jesus taught us to regard God as our loving, heavenly father. Any loving father is tickled pink when his children do well, because it reflects well on him. We can therefore be sure that God wants us all to be healthy, wealthy, and happy. Wise wouldn't hurt, either.

Putting It Together

New Thought history particularly extends from P. P. Quimby through Emma Curtis Hopkins and Malinda E. Cramer to the present. New Thoughters (who are frequently confused with New Agers, partly because many belong to both groups) tend to reject most occultism (psychic stuff) while embracing mysticism (direct experience of God).

You are a New Thoughter if you:

- Believe in a good God who is here and now available to us not only for inspiration and delightful direct experience but for thoroughly practical help.

- Believe that this divine goodness includes impartial, intelligent love extended toward all creatures, and utter reliability in responding to everyone.

- Believe that the universe is essentially mental or spiritual, however much we emphasize the part of it called material. *Whereas some, such as Christian Scientists, begin with the premise that God is all, and conclude that therefore matter is unreal, some New*

Thoughters begin with an assumed allness of God and conclude that therefore matter is spiritual. Everything is essentially mental-spiritual (experiential), and changing your thought and keeping it changed for the better can transform your life.

- Believe that God is all-inclusive (we and everything else are in God), but this inclusiveness does not make unreal the reality of individual selfhood and its freedom.

- Believe that there is no ultimately real and negative evil power in opposition to the good God. Evil is negative, a lack, like darkness, which is merely absence of light.

- Believe (and endeavor to put the belief to work in your life) that by the operation of your mind you can accept the goodness offered by God that requires your assent in order for God's purposes to become manifest in the human world.

- Believe that formal religion matters little in that no one religion or book contains truth to the exclusion of all others. *Many belong to a church or center, whether New Thought or traditional, for education, inspiration, association, and working together to accomplish various forms of good: personal, local, and worldwide.*

- Believe that Scripture may contain symbolic levels of meaning that are deeper than is obvious.

- Believe that people are essentially good, and that they have a spark of the divine. However, they don't always make good choices.

Chapter One

Not all New Thoughters subscribe to all the beliefs given here, and some New Thoughters add other beliefs. Some New Thoughters emphasize some beliefs and practices more than others. For some, New Thought is just a conviction that "as you believe, so you receive," with little theoretical buttressing of this, except for faith that there is a good, inspiring, accepting, reliable God who somehow makes everything work. For others, New Thought is a more developed theological outlook, including details about how the creative process proceeds.

In any event, New Thought can be characterized as the practice of the presence of God for practical purposes. You can practice the presence of God and be a mystic or a pietist, but not use your sense of the presence of God to bring about changes in your workaday world, and therefore not be a New Thoughter. You can pray to God to suspend some natural law and not be a New Thoughter, for New Thoughters believe that however miraculous a happening may seem, it reflects lawful order that we may not yet fully understand. What happens in your life depends on what you accept. You can believe, in a secular way, in the power of mind to accomplish much in life without being a New Thoughter, for New Thought insists on an immanent divine dimension to reality.

The essence of New Thought is belief in and use of the power of God-inspired mind over all circumstances. Some say that it is God responding to us in creating; others, that it is we responding to God in a direct process of cocreation.

New Thought's ancient roots mean that its principles have stood the test of time, which is a good start. But the human race is not through learning what is true and real, not by a long shot. So New Thought is "open at the top," as Religious Science founder Ernest Holmes put it, subject to constant revision in the face of new discoveries in science and new advances in philosophy, which is to say, sharper thinking. New Thought regularly rethinks and revises old ideas and adds new ones. Truth may turn up in all sorts of amazing places, for Truth, in much of New Thought terminology, is another name for God, who also turns up in all sorts of amazing places. More accurately, all sorts of amazing places turn up in God.

New Thought is largely based on the Bible and is Christian in the sense of following the teachings of Jesus. It also welcomes truth from other wisdom literature, but reminds you to be sure to put it to the test. What test? Jesus had a simple one: "Ye shall know them by their fruits" (Matt. 7:16). In other words, is following these principles getting you what you want? What you *really* want? (Did you ever get what you thought you wanted and find that it didn't meet your needs, so you weren't happy?) Are you deeply happy, healthy, and reasonably prosperous, or even unreasonably prosperous?

The Philosophy to be Tested

As a philosophy, New Thought falls into the metaphysical category of *idealism*. That means that it holds that the universe is made up of ideas, or thoughts, or spirit, or experiences. (The opposite of idealism is *materialism*, which holds that the universe is made up of matter, physical stuff, or lifeless energy.) Idealism would say that the physical is just a particular form of mental activity. The reason that this distinction is important is that if it's true that the world is made up of thoughts (at least for us rational animals), then it's possible for you to change the world with your thoughts, at least somewhat.

We can hear you protesting about all the times that your thoughts did not produce the desired results, or you got results that you had never thought about at all. Stay tuned. There are a couple of necessary pieces to be added to the New Thought model in addition to thoughts as the building blocks of the universe: what is the universe, and what or who is running it?

The basic concept underlying New Thought is that there is an infinite Good, an omnipresent, loving, intelligent Reality. We are all expressions of that One, but we are still individuals with a vital role to play in the process of cocreation, and all creation is cocreation. Now you can talk about Presence and Power, or Infinite Intelligence, or the Ultimate Absolute, or Utter Ineffability, or the Thing Itself, but it's easier to use the handy little three-letter word G-O-D. Here, too, you have to think things through for yourself, in case the three-letter word has negative overtones for you that you can't shake.

Philosophers have rumbled back and forth at each other for centuries with arguments for and against the existence of God and about the nature of God, whatever that means, but nobody is ever convinced by the arguments alone. People nearly always reach a conclusion based on their feelings and their personal experiences, not on their intellect. This may annoy some philosophers no end, but welcome to the real world.

New Thought holds that God, the ultimate power, is a power for good. There is no Satan, no evil personified. New Thought also holds that the universe is God's body. If God is good and God is everywhere available, then the universe must have good everywhere available in it. (We'll talk about evil at length in chapter 5. Yes, of course there is evil, but it isn't personified or even reified, "thingified." It is no-thing.)

Each of us human beings has free will, and we are therefore responsible for our choices. New Thought accepts the traditional Judeo-Christian teaching that we are made in the image and likeness of God. But unlike traditional teaching, New Thought holds that we are therefore inherently good, and we have never

Our Story Begins

lost our ability to choose the good. Although we are free to choose, we do not always choose wisely because of the influence of the past, and our choices are carrying us somewhere that may or may not be where we really want to go. Everyone else is also free to choose, and all those choosers are bound to come into conflict often. These intra- and inter-personal conflicts cause a great deal of difficulty for us. That means we still have a lot to learn, and God leads us through those learnings with infinite love and patience.

If everyone is to have free will and thereby be free to choose, then there has to be a neutral environment to choose in, an environment that does not favor one over another. God "sendeth the rain on the just and the unjust" (Matt. 5:45). Such an environment must operate lawfully, which means reliably, predictably; and so the universe has physical laws and mental laws, which are descriptions of how it operates. If we tailor our behavior to conform to these natural principles or laws, we can use them to get whatever we desire. This is how all the great advances of civilization have come about.

So go ahead and put this philosophy to the test. Test whether you in cooperation with God can use the power of your thoughts to change your world.

Some people have tried to leave belief in God out of the picture entirely and practice a distorted version of New Thought that is really an attempt to work one's will on the world without reference to any standard outside of oneself. This is a form of magic, and generally does not work well for long. Research has shown that human beings have a deep-seated need to believe in a power greater than themselves, and that those with such a belief heal faster and better from both mental and physical problems. Further, when the going gets rough, even if one subscribes to "humanistic" ethical principles, if one believes that there is no

Chapter One

God to turn to for help, what incentive is there to adhere to a arbitrary set of guidelines?

Many people ridicule New Thought teachings, believing that they are starry-eyed nonsense, Pollyanna, too good to be true. They are not familiar with the extensive research in physics, biology, and psychology that supports the power of the mind to influence the body and even to influence events and circumstances. Still others, stuck in outmoded religious beliefs, expect life to be miserable and painful because it is "God's will," and that those who prosper now will pay later in one way or another. These people are unaware of the abundance of the universe and God that is there for all to claim. Life is not a zero-sum game in which for you to win, another must lose, because the greatest wealth of all is the abundance of ideas. New Thought is definitely not too good to be true; its positive results can be obtained by anyone willing to exert the necessary mental self-discipline in conjunction with sufficient belief in a good God, leading, luring, and loving a friendly, abundant universe. In an abundant universe, all of us are entitled to all the abundance that we can develop the consciousness to attract.

New Thought in a nutshell is simple, but not at all easy. It is simple in that it consists of keeping your thoughts firmly fixed on what you want and off of what you don't want. However, this is the last thing that one is inclined to do when one is in difficulty of any sort, and so it is anything but easy. Many people read about the power of the mind, try to apply it in a casual, half-hearted way, and when they fail to achieve a desired result, say, "See, it doesn't work!" It works. They didn't. Or perhaps they pray to God as if God were a cosmic slot machine or celestial genie waiting to grant their prayers, forgetting that heaven helps those who help themselves. Or maybe they left God out of the picture altogether and tried to rely on their own puny efforts, not open to God's love, wisdom, and guidance, not working in harmony with universal principles, trying, like King Canute in the old story, to stop the tide from coming in. There he sat on his golden throne at the water's edge, issuing his royal command, and his feet all the while were getting wetter and wetter. (Some say that he anticipated this, and was using it to make his point.)

If you want to be healthy, wealthy, and happy, and you are willing to do what is necessary, you can be. Your health, wealth and happiness may look quite different from the health, wealth and happiness of the next person, because your desires are different. This is why nobody else can design a life for you: health, wealth, and happiness are definitely a do-it-yourself proposition. You have to visualize what you desire and then arrange your thoughts and energies accordingly, yet in harmony with universal principles, so that you prosper others as well as yourself. If you sincerely and wholeheartedly commit to this approach, and fine-tune it as necessary, you will become unstoppable. Seeming miracles happen to people who *make up their minds*, who change their thoughts and keep them changed.

Our Purpose

The purpose of this book is to describe the practice of the presence of God for practical purposes. We will examine each of the concepts bundled into this phrase, "the practice of the presence of God for practical purposes, and show how they work together to bring us health, wealth, and happiness.

First, we will examine the details of practice: what it means, and what it consists of. Next, we will take a look at what God and the universe must be like in order to be at all, i.e., look at the presence of God from the viewpoint of the philosopher and the mystic, with perhaps a bit of the theologian thrown in. As New Thought heads into the twenty-first century, it needs to update its

Chapter One

metaphysics to accommodate developments in science, particularly quantum physics; and developments in philosophy. At the same time, it must be careful to preserve the integrity of the original core ideas of the New Thought founders, and to remain in harmony with the teachings of Jesus. We present such an updated view, which we call *Process New Thought*.

Then, we will discuss specific practical daily-life purposes to achieve with our practice of the presence of God. These include health, wealth, happiness, relationships, and illumination or guidance.

Finally, we will provide some suggestions for what to do when things go wrong, which they invariably do from time to time. This will include a trip into the Black Hole of negativity, examining such concepts as sin, suffering, evil, fear, and just plain rotten personalities. But we shall not remain in the Black Hole; we include ways to get out of it quickly and peacefully. In fact, New Thought is really all about what you say to yourself when things go wrong, for it is then that you most need to be an optimist. Anybody can be a fair-weather sailor, but it takes strong character and self-discipline to weather the storms of life.

You are welcome to join us on our journey, where, as St. Paul told us, we can be transformed by the re*new*al of our minds (Rom. 12:2).

By mastering the complexities of today's world, we become capable of living longer and healthier lives, surrounded by material comforts while caring for the environment and relating harmoniously with each other in ways that ensure that everybody wins. Brother Lawrence could scarcely have dreamed of what has become possible for us today. And so we remain God-centered, adding to the practice of Brother Lawrence the God-aligned mental self-discipline of Quimby and the New Thought

Our Story Begins

denominational founders who succeeded him. Our techniques incorporate the approach developed by Stephen Covey, with bits of specific wisdom gleaned from many others along the way. To the simple joy of a monk we add the power of contemporary psychology, and get a balanced holism taking into account body, mind, emotions, and spirit.

Chapter One

2. Practicing

If we are to follow in the footsteps of Brother Lawrence and achieve the joy and contentment he found, we must follow his formula. The first ingredient is *practice*. Not just occasional practice, but a constant daily habit. Practic*ing*.

What is practice? The best definition of practice that we have seen (and we have forgotten where we saw it) is "a nontrivial activity undertaken on a regular basis primarily for its own sake." This is in contrast to the sort of practice that one does in order to get somewhere, such as Carnegie Hall.

Why should we practice? A practice such as Brother Lawrence's integrates and harmonizes body, mind, heart, and soul. It is transformative. It leads to positive, long-term, personal change.

How should we practice? Consistently, daily, habitually, automatically, so that we are doing it just like breathing. Before this can happen, we must have made a deliberate, carefully chosen decision to develop such a practice and sustain it until it becomes a habit.

New Thought, like Brother Lawrence, centers around one's thinking. Brother Lawrence managed to think about God all day long, often by conversing with him (for to Brother Lawrence, as to most of the Western mystics, God was masculine. Many Christian thinkers would agree with C. S. Lewis that in relation to God, we, i.e., our souls, are always feminine. Process thinkers and others today understand that God also has feminine qualities.) Since we become what we think about habitually, our practice will involve ways of shepherding our thoughts, mental activities that we repeat deliberately until they become second nature. These will teach us to habitually turn our attention toward what we want and away from what we don't want. Putting our attention on God gives us access to our creativity, allows us to create a day, to create a life, for creation is not confined to the arts.

New Thought minister Emmet Fox once gave, at Unity School of Christianity, a pair of lectures that were subsequently published as a booklet, *The Mental Equivalent*. Fox observed, "The aim of the metaphysical movement is to teach the practice of the presence of God. We practice the presence of God by seeing Him everywhere, in all things and in all people, despite appearances to the contrary." To see the presence of God is to see love, intelligence, health, peace, power, and beauty where others might see only difficulties. To do this, we must ride herd on our stray thoughts, and keep them from wandering off into fear or anger or discouragement. This mental self-discipline is one of the most difficult things we will ever do, yet it gives greater rewards than anything else we could ever undertake.

Mental equivalent is a term Fox says he borrowed from physics and chemistry (he was an electrical engineer before going into the ministry). In Fox's words,

> The secret of successful living is to build up the mental equivalent that you want; and to get rid of, to expunge, the mental equivalent that you do not want. . . . How do you do it? You build in the mental equivalents by thinking quietly, constantly, and persistently of the kind of thing you want, and by thinking that has two qualities: *clarity* or definiteness, and *interest*.

So we need to make clarity and interest habitual. We achieve clarity by visualizing what we want daily until the vision is clear. We get interested in what we are visualizing by learning all we can about it, and what impediments there may be between where we are and where we want to be. Then we use our creativity to get past the impediments. We develop skills, gather

Practicing

knowledge, and perform the necessary activities until our vision becomes a reality.

What Practice Involves

The one thing all of us really want is a relationship with God, the source of all good. So our practice will involve some sort of daily quiet time, when we allow our sense of God's presence to well up within us through prayer and meditation, along with some sort of inspirational reading, to help us develop our spirituality. Our practice will also involve some type of exercise for the body and for the mind, suited to our individual needs. And it will involve our interacting with other people by seeking first to understand, then to be understood (Covey's Habit Five), ensuring that everyone wins in every transaction (Habit Four), and working to synergize ideas and abilities into something better than either side could have come up with alone (Habit Six). We will need to determine which specific techniques are best for us. It is not enough just to agree intellectually that practice is a good idea; we must walk our talk. In short, our practice will be a collection of deliberately acquired habits involving our entire life viewed as a whole.

Any creative process is a cocreative process with God. God puts the brightest and best ideas into our minds. Stephen Covey likes to say that all things are created twice, first in the mind (like Fox's mental equivalent), then in the physical world. But not all creations are by conscious design. If we do not deliberately take control of our thinking and create our mental blueprint, we create by default from our own random thoughts or the thoughts of others, and we may not like the results we get. Because the subconscious mind cannot distinguish between fact and vivid imagination, mental rehearsal actually improves performance, as research in psychology has demonstrated. However, our goals must flow from and harmonize with our life's mission. If we adopt a few mental techniques in order to reach goals that are not part of an overall design for a life, we will not be integrated or congruent, and we will usually come a cropper. There's a big difference between *pretending* (living a lie), and *acting as if* (living in the blueprint), imagining what it will be like when the plan has become reality, and correcting as we go. We have to think carefully about what we really want, in consultation with God and in accordance with the universal principles that come from God, that are in harmony with the way the world works.

It's a funny thing about personal transformation: nobody can do it for you, not even God. As televangelist Robert Schuller puts it, "Even God can't steer a parked car." He also frequently emphasizes, "If it's going to be, it's up to me," which he regards as the heart of the Christian message. God is with you in every moment offering you wonderful possibilities for your life, but you have to accept them and get to work on them. God can help you in all sorts of ways, can orchestrate events so that things seem to fall into place for you, yet God has no hands but yours. Brother Lawrence engineered his own personal transformation by working to develop a habit of thinking about God, "the Father within," as Jesus put it, all day long as he did his chores. In this way, he was consulting with God in all that he did. He trusted God to guide him in little things as well as in big things. Once this became a habit, it was automatic, built into him, a part of him.

In a July 1997 article in *Guideposts*, the magazine's roving editor Elizabeth Sherrill tells of asking God about everything from which fork in the road to take when you are lost, to what food to eat in a Third World country where sanitation is questionable. Consulting God prior to taking action yourself is in sharp contrast to the old, childish approach of relying passively on God to dole out what you need with no thought or

Practicing

activity on your part. We, too, will be turning to God for guidance all day long; however, our partnership with God is an active one on both God's part and ours.

We aren't living in a monastery, with our lives regulated for us. Happily, we have much more freedom, but with that freedom comes responsibility for regulating our lives appropriately. We need some sort of guidelines, some principles on which to center our lives. New Thoughters find such principles in the teachings of Jesus. They can also be found in every other major religion and culture. Such principles are standards, external to us although they are implanted in us, that have been proven through the eons to work well. Living by them can bring us health, wealth, love, happiness, and overall success, not to mention inner peace. Stephen Covey sets them forth this way:

1. "The principle of continuous learning, of self-reeducation—the discipline that drives us toward the values we believe in." Conditions and circumstances change, and we must keep up with the changes if we are to lead satisfying lives. Formal schooling merely teaches us how to learn, but the real learning takes place once we get out into the everyday world.

2. "The principle of service, of giving oneself to others, of helping to facilitate other people's work." We are social animals, and it is in our best interest to look out for the interests of others. It also prospers us directly. As Robert Schuller puts it, the secret of success is to find a need and fill it.

3. "The principle of staying positive and optimistic, radiating positive energy—including avoiding the four emotional cancers (criticizing, complaining, comparing, and competing)." Positive optimism is one of the

Chapter Two

hallmarks of New Thought, and research in psychology clearly shows that optimists do better on just about any measure you care to name: health, success, longevity, schoolwork, getting elected to political office, and prosperity of all sorts.

4. "The principle of affirmation of others—treating people as proactive individuals who have great potential." To do this is to see the presence of God in others. It also sets up expectancy in the minds of all concerned, and extensive psychological research on expectancy shows that we generally get what we expect.

5. "The principle of balance—the ability to identify our various roles and to spend appropriate amounts of time in, and focus on, all the important roles and dimensions of our life. Success in one area of our life cannot compensate for neglect or failure in other areas of our life." Brother Lawrence had rather uncomplicated roles as monk, kitchen assistant, subordinate to the abbot, colleague to his fellow monks, and family member. For most of us, it is more challenging.

6. "The principle of spontaneity and serendipity—the ability to experience life with a sense of adventure, excitement, and fresh rediscovery, instead of trying to find a serious side to things that have no serious side." Religion—our beliefs, attitudes, and actions concerning our spirituality—too often becomes sober, weighty, and joy-killing. We can use our spirituality to create a lighthearted religion just as well. Jesus, after telling his disciples to keep his commandments about loving one another, concludes that they should do so "that your joy might be full" (John 15:11). The author of Proverbs had

it right: "A merry heart does good, like medicine, But a broken spirit dries the bones" (17:22).

7. "The principle of consistent self-renewal and self-improvement in the four dimensions of one's life: physical, mental, spiritual, and social-emotional." Covey illustrates this principle with a reference to the Aesop fable about the goose that laid golden eggs: Although you must take care of the eggs, you must also care for the goose, or you won't continue to be supplied with golden eggs for very long.

Centering your life on these principles external to the self and going beyond it, which serve as the North Star to steer by, according to Covey, is one of the great secrets of successful living. The principles have endured from age to age; they work. They are in harmony with the basic laws/cosmic habitforces of the universe, which come directly or indirectly from God. They underlie Covey's Seven Habits. The principles—and the habits based on them—are a guide to the choices that we make from moment to moment in all areas of our lives. Rather than respond to our moods or to expediency, we make our decisions in accordance with nomothetic (based on law) principles.

Practicing the presence of God combines nicely with the Habits. Both are undertaken for their own sake rather than to attain some other end. You don't do them to get promoted or to avoid hellfire or to placate your spouse; you do them because of the effect that they have on your life. (You may get promoted or your spouse may get placated anyway, and hell is a state of consciousness that you put yourself into and out of.) The Habits, coupled with a running conversation with God, include determining what you really want out of life and systematically going after it.

Chapter Two

...... in life depends in part upon interacting smoothly with other people, and putting emphasis on these smooth interactions is sometimes referred to as the personality ethic. Important as it is, it must rest on a firm foundation of character, the character ethic. This consists of traits such as courage, perseverance, honesty, and loyalty. In reviewing American success literature to create his Seven Habits model, Covey (like Huber) noted that after World War I, the character ethic, which is prominent in early New Thought literature and in the writings of Benjamin Franklin, was displaced by the personality ethic: winning friends and influencing people. To emphasize the personality ethic at the expense of the character ethic is to build the proverbial house on sand. The Seven Habits aid in the development of good character, with some attention also given to personality.

Covey's Seven Habits model has a maturity continuum from dependence to independence to interdependence. All of us start out dependent as infants on other people, and gradually develop independence. This is important growth, but the highest maturity, the greatest effectiveness, comes from interdependence, the harmonious synergy with others. Interdependence cannot occur until one is fully independent. So the first three Habits help us to develop independence, and then the next three help us to develop interdependence. The highest interdependence of all is our interdependence with God, and we'll say more about that in the next chapter.

Covey's first three Habits are:

1. *Be proactive.* Proactivity means that you don't wait for your ship to come in; you swim out to meet it. You assume responsibility for running your life, rather than leaving things to chance or seeing yourself as a victim.

As Covey puts it, you realize that you are the programmer of your life.

2. *Begin with the end in mind.* As the old saying goes, if you don't know where you're going, you'll probably end up somewhere else. What are you here for? What is your mission in life? What do you want on your tombstone? Pepperoni or anchovies? (Sorry, couldn't resist.) As the programmer, says Covey, you write the program. You assume leadership qualities of vision and imagination and set your course. Leadership ensures that you are doing right things, not just doing things right, which is management's function. Leadership has to come first. Otherwise, as Covey puts it, you might climb the ladder of success and discover that it is leaning against the wrong wall.

3. *Put first things first.* Nobody can manage time; it just keeps rolling along. What you can manage is your mind. You support your self-leadership through mind management. You run the program that you have written. By your choice of thoughts, you regulate your moods and motivation.

As a result of assuming responsibility for your life instead of remaining helpless, dependent, or victimized, you develop independence. You are then ready to develop the habits that will carry you to interdependence. However, life is lived in spirals. You will come past each habit many times, each time at a higher level of development and understanding. You don't have to have mastered the first three habits, which Covey calls the Private Victory, before you begin work on the second three, the Public Victory.

3. *Think win-win.* Not win-lose, or lose-win, or even compromise, where both sides lose a little. Everybody wins, or no deal. To live this habit, you must believe that this is an abundant universe with plenty for all, not a zero-sum game in which if one wins, another must lose. New Thought believes the Bible teachings about such an abundant universe.

4. *Seek first to understand, then to be understood.* As Covey observes, you need to diagnose before you prescribe. Endeavoring to understand the other person makes that person more willing to try to understand you. Such understanding is the major tool for achieving win-win outcomes.

6. *Synergize.* In synergy, the whole is greater than the sum of its parts because it includes the relationships among them. Synergy means that the combined efforts of two or more people lead to better outcomes than either or any could have achieved alone. You value the differences in people, because they are a resource. Covey remarks that if two of us see things exactly the same way, one of us is unnecessary.

Habit Seven is *Sharpen the saw*. On the diagram of Covey's model, it encircles the other habits. It comes from the old story about the man who, after trying for hours to cut down a tree with a dull saw, claims that he hasn't got time to sharpen it. This habit is about balance and renewal, about taking care of the goose that lays the golden eggs; about making sure that the physical, mental, emotional, and spiritual aspects of your life are in balance, with no aspect neglected in favor of the others.

Either we are free to succeed or to fail, or we are not free at all. We are responsible for our actions, and we take the

Practicing

consequences of them, good or bad. Covey says that if you pick up one end of the stick, you pick up the other end, too, meaning that although you are free to choose an action, you are not free from its consequences, because they come along automatically. This is the law of karma, or reaping what you sow, and it is the underlying law of the universe, applying to physical, mental, emotional, and spiritual realms alike. Covey talks about cramming in school: goofing off all semester, then staying up all night before an exam; and points out that it would never work to cram on a farm. Skip planting in the spring or watering in the heat of summer and then try to cram it all in just before harvest? Not exactly!

Karma, in Process New Thought terms, is the pattern of the past persisting into the present. If we begin to make a bacon-and-egg breakfast and then decide that we would really rather have pancakes, we still have to deal with the bacon and eggs sizzling away in the pan. The past therefore determines the present, but only in part. We can give the eggs and bacon to someone else, or throw them out, and have our pancakes. But it would be foolish for us to bewail the eggs and bacon, or feel victimized by them, even if someone else made them. We can't change the past, but we can make different choices in the present. And so our practice needs to be to ask what God recommends that we have for breakfast, for God always wants our highest good, and has a far better idea of what it is than we do, because God sees farther than we do. God frequently orchestrates events so that, say, a hungry person looking for bacon and eggs comes by at just the right moment.

Covey's books and tapes, particularly *The Seven Habits of Highly Effective People* and *First Things First*, explain the model and help with its implementation. Every New Thoughter, "brand name" or independent, ought to read, mark, learn, and

Chapter Two

inwardly digest this material not once, but repeatedly, for it is derived in large part from New Thought.

How to Get to Carnegie Hall

Apart from trying to get to Carnegie Hall, musical practice is the sort that we do for its own sake; we play because we love to play. Yet to reach a particular goal, we must make careful plans and let our practice support our efforts to carry them out.

No matter what we believe about God, or the Great Pumpkin, or however we conceptualize the Ultimate, if we want to have those beliefs support us in our day-to-day activities, we are going to have to think about God and our beliefs and bring our actions in line with those beliefs; and we are going to have to do it habitually. What's involved is mental self-discipline, and we are not going to be able or willing to put out the necessary effort to develop such discipline until and unless our beliefs make us feel that the game is worth the candle; otherwise, why bother? More about that in the next chapter.

Back to Carnegie Hall. If you are a would-be concert artist, you believe that it is possible for a human being to play a musical instrument beautifully. More than that, you believe that it is possible for you to play beautifully. You visualize yourself as a concert artist, but when you sit down at the keyboard or pick up the instrument, your initial efforts are anything but beautiful. Clearly, what is needed is a combination of knowledge and technique. So, you study harmony and counterpoint, and you practice your scales and chords, hour after hour, believing that all this work will result in the beautiful music that you imagine yourself creating. And you keep yourself encouraged by listening to records and tapes of great performances, or you attend live concerts to hear great musicians perform. Once in a while, you learn of a new fingering or memorizing technique,

Practicing

and you revise your approach accordingly. Music is what you do; you eat, drink, and sleep it. And with increasing frequency, you perform beautifully, and you begin to think of yourself as a concert artist.

Composer and creativity expert Robert Fritz has described his own struggles to learn to play the clarinet. He would wrestle with an étude for a week, then come in for a lesson and barely be able to play it. His smiling teacher would merely turn the page and assign the next étude. Then, some weeks later, the teacher turned back to the first étude. To Fritz's amazement, although he had not even looked at the piece in the meantime, he was able to play it easily and well. This is characteristic of our learning process as human beings. William James quoted a friend as saying that we learn to swim in the winter and to ice skate in the summer, meaning that the learning continues on a subconscious level.

The same is true of our struggles to create a beautiful life, one of abundance, of wellness, and of loving relationships. If we don't believe that we are capable of such performances, we will not attempt them. If we never sit down at the keyboard or pick up the instrument, we cannot expect to perform well; and if we allow ourselves to be buffeted by the winds of chance instead of designing and then executing the design for a good life, we won't have much to show for our years on this planet. If we cannot imagine what the music should sound like, we will not be very successful as musicians; and if we cannot picture what we desire for ourselves, we will not be able to bring it into existence.

None of this is new, and most of us have heard it before. But we somehow lapse back into the magical thinking of childhood, of expecting instant help, instant results, from the slightest effort at change on our part, like skipping one dessert and expecting to see a weight loss. This is partly the influence of

Chapter Two

our culture of fast foods and instant results, and it's partly a lack of character, specifically, patience and perseverance. We think we can do any old thing, any old way, and get a particular result; and if that result isn't immediate, we quit trying and switch to something else. Once in a while, we get lucky, and that only reinforces our belief in magical results from minimum effort. It's fine for a four-year-old to plant a lima bean in a paper cup full of dirt, then dig it up ten minutes later to see whether it has sprouted. It's not appropriate behavior for us as adults.

There's an old saying, "Chance favors the prepared mind." The same is true of miracles, which we have already defined as the operation of a natural law that as yet we do not understand. Miracles are not God suspending the rules just for us. Miracles are most likely to occur to the person with a miracle consciousness, one who expects a miracle and is prepared for it. And miracles are not always instantaneous. It took two years before Myrtle Fillmore, co-founder of Unity, was completely healed. With no doctor or drug intervention, her healing could well be called miraculous, since she was considered to be dying of hereditary tuberculosis. But Myrtle Fillmore displayed tremendous strength of character and mental discipline. Day in and day out for those two years, she maintained her focus on the idea, "I am a child of God, and therefore I do not inherit sickness." Her consciousness had been healed the day she grasped that idea. Now she had to bring all of her thinking and action in line with her new beliefs. She supplied her mind with reinforcement by reading the Gospels: She changed her eating habits and her speaking habits, saying only what she wished to be true and abandoning petty gossip. She did not succumb to "Oh, this will never work" thinking, or "Everybody says I'm crazy" thinking, or "This is taking too long" thinking. She kept her attention focused on what she wanted, believing in her partnership with God, who would do God's part in her healing if she would do hers.

Practicing
___

Any behavior (thinking, acting, or feeling) that we are not born with is learned. If it is learned, it can be unlearned. Still, old habits die hard, and it takes patience and perseverance to replace them with better habits. We have all accumulated a bunch of unconscious thinking (beliefs) that are not true or helpful, but they aren't going to go away on their own; we have to become aware of them and choose to drop them, replacing them with beliefs that serve us better. These unconscious beliefs include all sorts of notions about weakness, helplessness, or dependency, because we all start out as weak, helpless, dependent infants. Unfortunately, we aren't born with instruction books attached, and the vast majority of us do not receive the parenting we need, so we do not develop a sense of self-esteem, and we continue to look for someone or something outside ourselves, bigger, more powerful than we, to fight our battles for us. Or, worse, we give up on life, and substitute dependency on some substance for real living. The problem is compounded by religious beliefs in an omnipotent god to whom we relate as children, or worse, as serfs. Many fugitives from such toxic belief systems end up in New Thought churches, where all too often they find sympathy for their victimhood, a round of "Ain't it awful?," or codependence. All this only perpetuates the problem. Instead, we need to develop an adult relationship with a God who is reliable, loving, and intelligent. We need to take responsibility for our plight, become interested in it rather than dulled by it, as one English novelist put it. We need to change our thought and keep it changed, in Emmet Fox's words. And the only way to do this is to practice, and practice correctly, not practice a mistake.

Practicing correctly means first getting the procedure right, then repeating it over and over until doing it right becomes a habit, an unconscious competence. Or if we don't know what *right* is, experiment till we find out. If what you're doing isn't working, try *anything* else. What have you got to lose?

The key concept in all of this is our taking responsibility for our own lives, responsibility in the sense of response-ability, the ability to respond. As long as we are of sound mind, we are responsible, in all but the most extreme of circumstances, because no matter who did what terrible thing to us back then, we are able to respond now. In fact, we are the only ones who can respond in our own lives. The alternative is helplessness, giving up our freedom to others, as in a mental hospital or prison. In illness, poverty, or difficulties in relating to other people, we are still responsible for our own behavior. We are either helping our situation or hindering it by our thoughts, actions, and feelings.

But How Do I Do It?

Okay, so you're sold; you're responsible, you'll practice. But what are you practicing? How do you know what to practice, when your life is in a shambles and nothing you do seems right? Well, what do you want? What do you *really* want, not what do you think will temporarily ease your pain, or make you happy, which nothing outside of you can ever do? What you are practicing is the shift of your attention from what you don't want to what you do want. As in training a puppy, the mind has to be pulled back over and over again from dwelling on the negative, from ruminating and obsessing over lack and limitation instead of concentrating on what is left, what is available, what is possible in this universe of abundance. You will only be willing to make and sustain the necessary effort to do this when you believe deep down that you have a solid partnership with the one and only good God, whom you can rely on, that this partnership is the source of all that you could ever need in the form of ideas and connections with other people and resources, and that this partnership functions in an abundant and neutral universe that operates lawfully and dependably. In such a universe, you take the credit when you do well and the blame

Practicing

when you mess up, knowing that you are always free to learn and to try again. You may make mistakes, but you are not a mistake.

Despite appearances, the universe is a level playing field. We don't know what is in another person's consciousness; the other person may not know what is in his or her unconscious. We can't see far enough into the future to know how certain apparently negative circumstances may be working out for the highest good of all concerned. We can't see far enough into the past to know whether someone is experiencing the effects of his or her actions in a previous lifetime, let alone know whether indeed there were previous lifetimes. We can't even remember what we did last week! But God sees farther than we do. God offers perfect possibilities for us right now, adjusted to take into account everything that has happened up until now. We probably aren't even certain what we are in this lifetime to learn, but God knows. Our job is to figure out what we really want and go after it, steadily, intelligently, with love and enthusiasm.

Now, please notice that nobody is saying anything about pretending that things are peachy when they're putrid, denying that current reality is the way it is. In New Thought, denial means "No, I don't have to accept that." Denials are always followed by affirmations: "I choose this instead," so we don't leave a vacuum into which weed seeds can drift, random ideas that may or may not be in our best interests, seven other spirits more wicked than the first, as in Jesus's parable (Luke 17:26). And here's the trick: you have to mean what you are saying. You have to believe it deep down, in a heartfelt way, not just *want* to believe what you're saying, or agree intellectually with what you're saying. You can't just wish for what feels good without listening for what your higher self has to say about it. Is your wish really in your best interest, or for the highest good of all concerned? Is there any good reason why you should not

Chapter Two

have what you want? What would your life be like if you got it? Would you really want that kind of life? Do you really want the headaches that go with, say, being President of the United States? There have been many cynical comments about answered prayers that one later wished had gone unanswered! And there have been many people who went off half-cocked after some wishful thinking that wasn't sufficiently thought through, quitting a despised job prematurely, telling someone off imprudently, marrying in haste and repenting at leisure. You have to leave God some wiggle room to guide you in tailoring your plans so that they are just right for you, to give you perfect possibilities for your current situation.

An Adult Partnership

We are working to avoid two extremes: leaving everything up to God on the one hand, and trying to do everything ourselves on the other. We need to find the middle ground of partnership, with God as our senior partner, the one who sees farther, who is the source of everything. We are adult partners, and we hold up our half of the log. This means that we value ourselves and our desires. We have self-esteem: a trust in our own abilities that is based on character and competence, as Stephen Covey puts it; and we are in charge of developing both. Character is the collection of habits that make us dependable, honest, courageous, persistent, and loyal. Competence is a high level of proficiency in one or more valuable skills. Nobody else conveys character and competence to us; they are an inside job. We work to develop them, and we practice behaving as we believe we should. We decide how to act, and then act that way consistently.

Some of the best help in establishing an adult relationship with God comes from Father Leo Booth, the aforementioned Episcopal priest and New Thoughter. His book, *The God Game:*

Practicing

It's Your Move, tells about the limiting religious beliefs we pick up in childhood and how to get rid of them. New Thought is rife with fugitives from toxic religions, most of whom are stuck in childish patterns of interacting with God. New Thought principles are like water on parched earth to them: the freedom to believe as we like, with no authority riding herd on us. New Thoughters, in their desire to help, do not challenge these newcomers, who frequently think that New Thought is about believing any old thing you want any old way you want, and Santa God will magically come through when you put your penny of belief in the cosmic slot machine. Then these newcomers are crestfallen when it doesn't work for them, thinking they aren't "good enough," or "spiritual enough," or they just didn't believe hard enough, or worse, that it is all a lot of hooey. But the arthritis didn't go away, or they didn't win the lottery, or Prince Charming hasn't shown up.

The two commonest mistakes in practice are not being clear and consistent, and giving up too soon. Emmet Fox says that if you are trying to do time lapse photography of a vase, and you jerk it away and replace it with a bunch of flowers, then a top hat, you will not get good results. This is true of our spiritual/mental work as well. Decide what you want and stay with it until you get it. This doesn't mean you can't fine-tune your practice, can't improve the details of your plan. Just don't be all over the place. Slow and steady wins the race. In the rare situations where you actually need to be fast and versatile, you will have developed those talents by careful practice, or you won't be in that situation. New Thought author Florence Scovel Shinn tells of doing a treatment (prayer work) for someone who negated all that she did by grumbling about how it was never going to work. As our friend Jane Elizabeth Allen puts it, "Your brain hears what your mouth says!"

Chapter Two

Getting In the Habit

Interesting things happen to people who practice certain kinds of activities habitually. They go into a flow state that is an altered state of consciousness in which they feel at one with the universe and at peace. They may experience time distortion of a sort associated with hypnotic trance. And they experience so much pleasure that they become positively addicted to their practice, in much the way that one becomes negatively addicted to certain substances. This positive addiction is the result of the release of brain chemicals such as endorphins and encephalins.

Runners frequently become positively addicted, as do meditators. Psychiatrist William Glasser in his book *Positive Addiction* describes people who became positively addicted to knitting, chanting, and even a late-afternoon bike ride!

Large amounts of habitual practice result in what is known as overlearning, learning so firmly entrenched that it can be counted on even under stressful conditions when one might not expect to perform at one's best. Then one is able to come through in a crunch. We once heard a story about a famous baseball player who as a youngster spent hours down in the family basement swinging a bat at a rope with two knots in it to indicate the top and bottom of the strike zone. He was renowned for being able to come through with a hit when his team needed it the most. Another story tells of a famous brain surgeon whose father, hearing strange sounds in the night, walked into the darkened family kitchen to find his adolescent son tying knots in a string draped over a kitchen chair, explaining that as a brain surgeon, he would have to be able to tie knots in the dark. This sort of overlearning is what the practice of the presence of God gives us, so that in the crunch, we instinctively turn to God for guidance, in quiet confidence that things will work out well. If we wait until we are in a pickle and then try to pray, or develop a

Practicing

set of unifying principles to live by, we will find it much harder going. This is why schools have fire drills.

So we need to have a practice that we undertake deliberately and with great thought, a collection of habits that we rehearse over and over on a daily basis, once we have determined that these are what we intend to run our life around. There is very little that we can't improve with practice, even if we lack natural aptitude.

Covey explains, as background to his first three Habits, that taking responsibility for your life makes you aware that you are the programmer of your life. You therefore undertake to write a program for your life, a mission statement that you intend to live by and from which all your goals flow. Then, by putting first things first, prioritizing your activities, you run the program. This program is your practice. It involves your conversations with God, your weekly planning, and your way of dealing with the people and situations in your life (Habits Four, Five, and Six). It also involves your efforts to support your beliefs.

All We Like Sheep Have Gone Astray

Your main task is the habitual shepherding of your thoughts, which is how you bring your performance in line with your chosen principles. All too often, thoughts, like sheep, stray off onto negative subjects and remain caught there. There are two techniques you can use to bring them back: disputation, and pattern interruption. *Disputation* is the technique used by Quimby and by Myrtle Fillmore, and consists of arguing with a negative idea. This technique appears in the Rational-Emotive Therapy of psychiatrist Albert Ellis. For example, if you come out of work and find that you have a flat tire, you may go off into an orgy of negativity, angrily declaring this to be catastrophic. Disputing this would be pointing out to yourself that while this situation may be annoying and inconvenient, it is hardly catastrophic, your life is not threatened by it, and you probably have several choices available to you as remedies. As you mentally or even orally rehearse such rational thoughts, the negative, overreacting thoughts begin to dissipate.

Pattern interruption is anything that abruptly distracts you and breaks your mental pattern. Some people slam a hand on the table or a fist against the wall (which can be hard on the wall and is not recommended). This is accompanied by saying "No!" in a loud, firm voice. A gentler but equally effective method is to wear a wide rubber band on your wrist and snap it every time you catch yourself ruminating on a bunch of negative thoughts.

Another way to shepherd your thoughts is by *reframing*. This means to put a different frame around a situation as if it were a picture, to view it in a different and more positive light. For example, if your boyfriend or girlfriend dumps you, you might at first be devastated by the thought that you are unlovable. Reframing that thought, you would rejoice to have that unappreciative person out of your life so that you were free to attract a person who would appreciate all your fine qualities. It's a variant of the old "is the glass half empty or half full" routine.

Thought shepherding is closely related to *mood control*. We need to develop the ability to shift quickly from an unempowering state to a powerful frame of mind. This is done by carefully and deliberately choosing helpful, positive thoughts to dwell on in the present moment, and by assuming a supportive body posture. You say to yourself, "I won't think about negative outcomes; I will think about positive ones." We have all done this kind of shifting at one time or another: suppose you are having a heated argument with someone and the doorbell rings. Most of us would manage to quickly shift our mood to at least

Practicing

---

neutral, if not pleasant, for the sake of the innocent person at the door.

A discouraged person sits with head bowed, slumped, frowning. An upbeat, powerful person sits erect, with head held high, looking and acting energetic. If you fake an energy you do not feel for a few minutes, you will begin to feel energetic. If you paste on a fake smile and hold it, you will presently begin to feel happier. The mind-body connection works both ways. Besides, as some wag has observed, a fake smile is preferable to a sincere frown. However, this practice is only of limited usefulness unless you are proactive and have assumed responsibility for your life by working out a mission statement and aligning your thoughts and behavior with God and God's universal principles.

It is literally true that to an enormous extent, we build our world with our thoughts, for thoughts can influence the movement of subatomic particles. Once we really make up our minds to do something, the entire universe seems to rally to our aid. Critics, even when they are close family members, tend to become silent once they realize that we are dedicated to a particular undertaking. Oh, they may grumble a little now and then, but they usually withdraw their opposition once it becomes clear that we have thoroughly thought through what we intend to do and are committed to it with no internal doubts or conflicts of our own.

Barbara Sher, in her book *Teamswork*, illustrates repeatedly how a roomful of strangers can help each other achieve their heart's desire. There is always somebody who has an uncle who runs a business, or knows a guy with a truck, or is good at a particular skill that is needed; and suddenly, the impossible dream is not only possible, it is on track and on the way to you. But first, you have to overcome the fear thoughts, the self-doubt, the discouragement, and the conflicting beliefs that are often unconscious.

Changing Beliefs

One of the main practices that make up our practice needs to be taking responsibility for what we believe deep down, rather than just what we give intellectual assent to. Therapist Robert Dilts was the assistant to the founders of neuro-linguistic programming (NLP), the study of the effects of language—both verbal and non-verbal—on the central nervous system. In his book, *Beliefs: Pathways to Health and Well-Being*, he tells of working with his mother, who had metastasized breast cancer, which her doctors considered terminal. For four long days, he worked with her beliefs about herself and her illness, using numerous NLP techniques and stopping only for her to eat or sleep. Dilts explains,

> I assisted my mother in changing a number of limiting beliefs and helped her integrate major conflicts that had developed in her life because of all the life changes that had occurred. As a result of the work we did with her beliefs, she was able to make dramatic improvements in her health and elected not to receive chemotherapy, radiation treatment, or any other traditional therapy. At the time of the writing of this book (7 years later) she is in excellent health, and there have been no further cancer symptoms. She swims one-half mile several times per week and is living a happy full life that includes trips to Europe and roles in TV commercials. She's an inspiration for all of us about what is possible for people with life-threatening illnesses.

Practicing

Even with useful techniques, people sometimes hold beliefs that somehow negate the change they desire. Dilts tells of a schoolteacher who loved the NLP strategy for becoming a good speller, and used it on all her students, but complained that it didn't work for her personally. Dilts found that she could indeed learn the strategy, but because she didn't *believe* that she could spell, she would discount her new ability, thereby allowing herself to override all the evidence that she was indeed able to spell. He states,

> Belief systems are the large frame around any change work that you do. You can teach people to spell as long as they're alive and can feed back information. However, if people really believe they can't do something, they're going to find an unconscious way to keep the change from occurring. They'll find a way to interpret the results to conform with their existing belief. In order to get the teacher . . . to use the spelling strategy, we'd have to work with her limiting belief first.

Dilts outlines the steps for creating change:

1. Identify the present state.
2. Identify the desired state.
3. Identify the appropriate resources (internal states, physiology, information or skills) that you need to get from present state to desired state; and
4. Eliminate any interferences through using those resources.

He sums up, "You've got to *want* to change, *know how* to change, and give yourself the *chance* to change." Frequently, some part of you doesn't want to change because of some positive benefit gained from the problem behavior. This internal saboteur can interfere with your plans. Or you may not know how to picture your desired change, or how you'd behave if you did change. Or you may not have allowed enough time or space for change to take place, not given yourself a chance to change.

Outcome expectancy means that you believe that your *goal* is achievable. Without it, you feel hopeless, and you won't take appropriate action. *Self-efficacy expectancy* means that you believe that *you* are able to achieve your goal. Without it, you feel helpless. If you feel both hopeless and helpless, according to Dilts, you become apathetic. We tend to get what we expect, good or bad.

Beliefs, Dilts claims,

> are not necessarily based upon a logical framework of ideas. They are, instead, notoriously unresponsive to logic. They are not intended to coincide with reality, Since you don't really know what is real, you have to form a belief—a matter of faith.

There's an old story about a psychiatrist treating a man who believed he was a corpse, despite all logical arguments to persuade him that he was alive. Finally, the psychiatrist, in a burst of inspiration, asked his patient, "Do corpses bleed?" "Of course not; that's ridiculous!" replied the patient. So the psychiatrist, after receiving permission, pricked the man's finger and out came a drop of bright red blood. Looking at his bleeding finger with astonishment, the patient exclaimed, "I'll be damned, corpses *do* bleed!"

Often, simply becoming aware that you are holding a belief that is not useful to you is enough to enable you to replace it with a better belief. If you believe that you are a corpse, past hope, you won't be inclined to do what is necessary to overcome an

Practicing

---

illness. Once you recognize and challenge that belief, healing often comes speedily.

Much of our practice consists of the maintenance of a positive attitude. Dilts comments,

> Positive attitudes are not steady states. If you wake up on the wrong side of the bed and have a major fight with your spouse or you have some problems at work, it may feed into your doubts. On the other hand, somebody who makes a major belief change and then opens herself up and gets into new relationships or improves her old ones will reinforce her positive attitude. She'll set up a self-reinforcing loop, so she is constantly, positively reinforced.

Dilts also remarks, "Changing beliefs is not necessarily a long, arduous, painful process." It doesn't necessarily have to take even as long as the four days that he spent working with his mother. Each person is different because each person's needs are different.

Practice as the Path

George Leonard, author of *Mastery*, believes that practice is not something you *do*, but something you *have*, something you *are*. "In this sense," he maintains, "the word is akin to the Chinese word *tao* and the Japanese word *do*, both of which mean, literally, road or path. Practice is the path upon which you travel, just that." Since Dilts sees beliefs as pathways, our beliefs can be seen as part of our practice, part of what we are. There's an old saying that if you believe you can, or you believe you can't, you're right.

Chapter Two

Having assumed responsibility for our life and determined our overall mission, what techniques might be helpful in our practice? Having set goals that flow from our mission, how can we remain principle-centered and reach them?

First, remain open-minded and ready to learn. This is an attitude, but choosing it habitually is a technique. Unity minister Edwene Gaines affirms, "I'm teachable!" Emmet Fox says that you must be absolutely firm and unwavering in your belief during a spiritual treatment and open to new ideas the rest of the time, an important distinction. People are where they need to be to learn what they need to learn, and you are no exception. This continuous learning principle is one of those mentioned by Stephen Covey and by business management consultant Peter Senge in his book, *The Fifth Discipline*, in which he writes about organizations dedicated to lifelong learning. Such learning includes academic subjects as well as interpersonal skills and other psychological knowledge. Senge observes, "Personal mastery is the discipline of continually clarifying and deepening our personal vision, of focusing our energies, of developing patience, and of seeing reality objectively."

Other attitudes included in our practice are the attitude of gratitude, noting what we have to be grateful for and expressing our thanks to God and to other people. This puts our attention on what we have to be thankful for, and since what you give your attention to grows, it tends to attract more to be thankful for! We have already mentioned maintaining a positive attitude, and looking for and expecting the best from people and situations.

Prayer and meditation are time-honored techniques for developing spirituality, and they should be the cornerstones of our practice. Prayer has been described as talking to God and meditation as listening to God. Prayer includes prayers of asking and prayers of thanksgiving, prayers of praise and prayers of

Practicing

denial. One of the great Christian mystics remarked that if one's only prayers were prayers of thanksgiving, one would do well indeed. However, Jesus said, "Ask, and it shall be given you" (Matt. 7:7), not because God doesn't already know, but because in order to ask, you must be clear in your own mind about what you want. Prayers don't have to be formal or fancy, unless you happen to like them that way. God doesn't stand on ceremony.

There are numerous forms of meditation that have in common the quieting of mind and body in various ways. With calm and relaxation, the still, small voice of God is easier to hear. Many people find it easier to meditate in a natural setting, and those who find it difficult to sit still may enjoy a walking meditation in a woods or garden. Unity co-founder Charles Fillmore called his form of meditation "sitting in the silence," waiting for God to speak to him. Eastern techniques involve regulating the breath in order to relax the body, and research by physician Herbert Benson and others has confirmed the physical benefits of such practice. Experiment with an open mind until you find what works well for you. Prayer and meditation figured prominently in Brother Lawrence's practice.

Affirmation is sometimes classified as a form of prayer. Whatever you call it, a good affirmation is a useful blueprint. Affirmations should be *I* statements, in the present tense, and positive, because the subconscious mind has difficulty processing negatives, and it experiences only the present. Because the subconscious mind functions as a servomechanism, and because it cannot distinguish between fact and vivid imagination, it immediately goes to work to make your perception of reality match your affirmed statement of it, unless something else, such as an old belief, interferes.

Mindlessly parroting affirmations over and over, or plastering them all over the refrigerator, does little good.

Chapter Two

Mindful repetition, however, oral or written, noticing your own inner objections as they arise, can be helpful. You can either dispute the objection or just let it sit there and glower while you repeat the affirmation, a sort of broken-record technique.

There are also special affirmations such as "Divine order" that serve to turn your attention to where it belongs and off of your difficulty. Other favorites are "Peace, be still," and Unity minister James Gaither's contribution, "Lighten up!" *Creative Thought*, *Daily Word*, and *Science of Mind* all offer daily affirmations. Other affirmations can be found in *New Thought* and in the writings of many New Thought authors, notably Catherine Ponder, whose affirmations frequently get quoted by other authors. Ponder, in turn, got some of hers from Florence Scovel Shinn. A good affirmation tends to travel as far and fast as a good story.

Reading inspirational material is a wonderful technique to use as a regular practice. Then when the going gets rough, stories about people who have succeeded in overcoming various difficulties tend to come to your mind and encourage you. Reading the Bible and symbolic interpretations of it are enormously helpful. Emmet Fox and Catherine Ponder are two New Thought authors who have written extensively about symbolic interpretation of Scripture. The *Science of Mind* textbook of Religious Science, written by founder Ernest Holmes, includes symbolic interpretations of some stories and parables from the Bible.

Finally, modeling (emulating) excellent spiritual performers is a superb technique for developing your own spirituality. To model someone, you need to know the person's beliefs, syntax (the order and method of procedure), and physiology. Then, you imitate the person as closely as possible.

Practicing

The ideal person to model is Jesus, and we know a lot about his beliefs, syntax, and physiology. He believed in God as his loving Father within, and in an abundant universe. He gave thanks in advance when he prayed. He lifted his eyes to heaven rather than going around downcast. And he spent a lot of time in prayer and meditation.

We might also want to model Emmet Fox, who has helpfully supplied the information we need in the form of his Golden Key. When you are in any sort of difficulty, he teaches, you must somehow manage to stop thinking about the difficulty and start thinking about God instead. You do this by rehearsing all that you know about God: God's omnipresence, loving dependability, etc. You can rehearse appropriate passages from the Bible: "If God be for us, who can be against us?" (Rom 8:31), or "Before they call, I will answer, and while they are still speaking, I will hear" (Isa. 65:24), or "God is our hope and strength, a very present help in time of trouble" (Ps. 46); or just talk to God in some fashion. Then you release all concern about the outcome of the difficulty for as long as possible, resuming your daily activity. If the fear or worry thoughts return, you remind yourself that you have already "Golden Keyed" the situation, and continue to think about God. Fox assures us that if we sustain this, we will rapidly find that we are somehow out of danger or difficulty, often in amazing ways.

Other people to model are characters in the Bible, other literary figures, and living models such as Stephen Covey, who describes his beliefs, syntax, and physiology in his books. New Thought minister and "boss angel" on television's *Touched by an Angel* Della Reese has overcome numerous difficulties by practicing the presence of God with deep, unwavering faith coupled with an equally deep sense of humor. God and Della are very tight, honey! New Thought minister Mary Morrissey describes health, financial, and relational challenges that she has overcome in her book, *Building Your Field of Dreams*.

Dilts notes,

> When you interview people that are very good at something, it is common for them to have a clear, highly detailed representation of whatever it is they do well. They represent their successes vividly. When you ask them about their failures, they often have vague representations of those and there is hardly any physiological response.

Those that have ears to hear, let them hear.

Summary

To recapitulate, our practice consists of first contemplating God in the silence; then visualizing what we want, making plans, and carrying them out, all with God's guidance. We communicate with God constantly, both talking and listening. Our stance is always proactive. We develop a mission statement for our lives, revising it from time to time as appropriate, and make sure that all our goals and activities are in harmony with that mission statement and flow from it. Then, in our daily activities, we put first things first, giving priority to meeting our goals, acting in harmony with universal principles, and remembering that people are more important than things. We seek to understand others before trying to be understood on our way to a win-win outcome in all our transactions. Our attention is on solutions, not on problems. Our plans may have to change as we learn more or encounter other human beings with needs that we can and should meet. We make these changes in accordance with universal principles. We include in our plans attention to physical, mental, social/emotional, and spiritual

Practicing

aspects of life, assuring that these aspects remain balanced in our lives.

All the while, we quietly affirm that what we desire has already come to pass, and we give thanks for it in advance, as Jesus did. Even in our desiring, by giving thanks to God, we are practicing the presence of God.

Chapter Two

3. The Presence of God

We are happy to announce, following Mark Twain, that the reports of God's demise are greatly exaggerated. God is alive and well and everywhere present in the universe, doing exactly what God is supposed to be doing. As we have already mentioned, many, if not most of us grow up with weird notions about God that we have acquired, partly because of our perspective as helpless little children in a world of powerful adults, and partly because of toxic religious teachings.

What we would like to do in this chapter is give you a wonderful, positive, science-correlated, up-to-date, synergized view of God. We continue to use the term *God* to refer to this Ultimate Being, partly so that you can overwrite any negative views of God that may still be bumping about in your subconscious mind creating mischief, and partly because it is a handy little three-letter word. It does not have to imply masculinity or indeed gender at all. This view is a blend of philosophical *personalism* (God is the ultimate person, not a limited human personality or giant human being), *panentheism* (all is in God), and *process thought* (everything is made of experiences, and God is a personally ordered society of experiences). We'll explain in a moment. But first, a word from our sponsor, organized religion.

Organized religion is good news and bad news. The good news is that the best way to ensure the perpetuation of anything worthwhile is to institutionalize it. The bad news is that the quickest way to distort, stifle, rigidify, or embalm anything worthwhile is to institutionalize it. As William James once remarked, "No priesthood ever initiated its own reform." So, although we don't want to condemn all organized religion, prudence dictates that we take each one apart and examine it dispassionately and logically, while seated in the philosopher's armchair, wearing our philosopher's hat. When you remove the emotion that accompanies many religious beliefs like a cloud of incense, some of them prove to be as naked as the emperor in his new clothes, to mix metaphors. Or worse, they lead straight to atheism, which is not helpful.

This may sound like a lot of bother, and it is. So why bother? For three reasons: the **first** is that God is the centerpiece of Brother Lawrence's masterpiece, and if we want to reap the same benefits that he did, we need to model his beliefs, so we had better take a close look at them. The **second** reason is that as we have already mentioned, research in psychology has shown overwhelmingly that people who believe in a power greater than themselves get along better in life. Presumably, belief in the Tooth Fairy would suffice, but we trust that you, gentle reader, are farther along the path than that. The **third** reason is that your view of God affects your view of healing, prosperity, and yourself in general. Can you count on God, or are you at God's whim? Or worse, do you see God as having no power to assist you?

In order to find the courage to persevere with our practice in the face of the difficulties that inevitably arise in any life, we need an understanding of the nature of God and of the universe. Then we can develop our relationship with God as we would with a loving and wise parent, a senior partner to whom we regularly turn for advice, comfort, and encouragement. God loves us and wants only our highest good. As Unity author Emilie Cady puts it, "Desire in the heart is always God tapping at the door of your consciousness with His infinite supply." God is good, and the universe, as God's body, expresses much of God's goodness.

In New Thought, people are free to believe whatever they choose. However, since nearly all the original New Thought leaders came from a Western Christian background, its teachings are based on the teachings of Jesus, though not necessarily the teachings about Jesus. Further, Jesus was a Jew, and Mohammed was influenced by his teachings. The three great Western religions are Judaism, Christianity, and Islam, so we as Westerners would be foolish to discard or overlook this rich source of wisdom. Even the Dalai Lama states, in his book, *The Good Heart: A Buddhist Perspective on the Teachings of Jesus*:

> It is my full conviction that the variety of religious traditions today is valuable and relevant. According to my own experience, all of the world's major religious traditions provide a common language and message upon which we can build a genuine understanding. In general, I am in favor of people continuing to follow the religion of their own culture and inheritance. . . it is better to experience the value of one's own religious tradition. . . If you are Christian, it is better to develop spiritually within your religion and be a genuine, good Christian. If you are a Buddhist, be a genuine Buddhist. Not something half-and-half! This may cause only confusion in your mind.

As a religious movement that originated in the nineteenth century, New Thought up until now has rested on nineteenth-century metaphysics. Like Newtonian physics, older views of metaphysics are becoming increasingly out of step with the world of today. It is time for New Thought to update its metaphysics, including taking a fresh look at its ideas about God.

We propose to follow a path that leads between traditional theism and classical pantheism and attempts to bring them together. It is a path that keeps us up to date with contemporary science, using philosophy as a balance point between science and mysticism. We call it the path of the three p's: personalism, panentheism, and process. But first, a word about metaphysics.

Chapter Three

Metaphysical Metamorphosis

In philosophy, the systematic study of what all things visible and invisible are really like is known as *metaphysics*. It got this name because in the arrangement given to Aristotle's writings after his death, the writings on what he called *first philosophy* were placed *meta ta physica*, meaning *after* the writings on physics. In the nineteenth century, people in New Thought and related outlooks began using the term *metaphysics* to refer to their practical philosophy, which emphasized what was *beyond* physics, especially beyond the visible world. But metaphysics in the original sense is concerned with what underlies both the physical and nonphysical. Unhappily, the secondary meaning of metaphysics as "esoteric, often mystical or theosophical, lore" has crept, or should we say slithered, into dictionaries and seems to be here to stay, but it still makes philosophers twitchy, because it is confusing.

In the twentieth century, metaphysics—in the original sense—has become unfashionable. One ray of sunshine in the murk is the work of Alfred North Whitehead, the celebrated mathematician who turned from mathematics and physics to pursue philosophy, specifically, a system of metaphysics that takes into account twentieth-century physics.

Things seem solid to our physical senses, yet even some of the ancient Greeks knew that the world was not a solid mass, but rather was made of atoms. Quantum physicists tell us that the universe is not static substance, as it appears to be, but dynamic, ever changing, existing as momentary bursts of energy that they call *quanta*. Whitehead called these quanta *occasions of experience*, and as he studied the world from his philosopher's armchair, he concluded that they are all living, not lifeless energy, as the scientists had supposed.

The Presence of God

Aggregations or societies of these experiences form you, us, and everything that exists; and they continue to do so moment by moment, in ongoing bursts of *living* energy. The aggregation of experiences that we call a rock is not alive, but the experiences that compose it are. This view of the world as dynamic is called a *process* view, in contrast to a *substance* view that sees reality as enduring substance underlying change. According to process thought, experiences do not change, but they come very quickly, one right after another, each a little different from its predecessor. Each experience then becomes part of the past, influencing each succeeding experience at least a tiny bit.

Whitehead further realized, as he studied the world, that the only way he could account for novelty, departing from the pattern of the past, was by the presence of God. The son of an Anglican priest, Whitehead had at one time spent eight years studying theology, then abruptly ceased, and sold his theology books. So it was not lightly or casually that he reintroduced the notion of God into his metaphysics, and considered what the nature of God must be. He concluded that not only is the world composed of living energy coming in bursts, or experiences, but in each experience, God is present, offering perfect possibilities that are particularly relevant to that experience at that time; the orientation that God offers to an experience is called its initial aim. The experience chooses between this and the pattern of the past, emphasizing either to some extent that it selects. We are literally new every moment, with a new opportunity to make a fresh start.

Without the activity of God, possibilities never would be translated into actuality, something that those who claim that the ultimate is pure potentiality seem not to realize. Process theologian Marjorie Suchocki, in her book, *God Christ Church: A Practical Guide to Process Theology*, states,

Chapter Three

All possibilities have their locus in God. The only limitation upon actualization of particular kinds of possibilities would appear to be the constructive limitation of existence itself—for if God is to exist, the possibilities must be unified. Unification is order and valuation in terms of harmony—the terms are almost synonyms with one another. The implication is that for God to exist—for the infinite possibilities to be localized at all—God must be good. God, by self-definition, must be good, for if God were not a unification, a harmonization, of all possibilities, God simply would not be.

We have free will; therefore, we can decide how much of God's possibilities we choose to accept and how much of the pattern of the past we choose to continue, so that at each moment we are blending the past with the possible. We choose, each moment, and all our choices are carrying us in some direction. If we accept God's loving and wise guidance, it will be in the direction of our highest good.

With all of us choosing, there are inevitably conflicts between choosers, and even between some of our own choices. Still, God is always working to mitigate things that go wrong, orchestrating events by offering possibilities in ways that lead toward greater good. God, as we have already noted, is the source of the principles that are universally recognized as wise and good ways to live. Under God's guidance, the physical laws—habits of interaction—evolved to constitute a neutral environment in which to exercise our free will, a level playing field. So we have God's unconditional love, balanced by the benefits of working in accordance with the habitforces of the universe or the consequences of breaking them. We are punished by our sins, not for them, and we are free in the next moment to accept God's loving guidance and not make the same mistakes.

We do have problems, which we sometimes realize are opportunities in disguise. What we may not realize is that with no problems, no challenges, we would all be bored to death. Teamed up with God, who sees farther than we do, we can solve the problems, provided that we keep our attention focused on solutions instead of on the problems. We have to use our practice to keep centered on God and on what we want, knowing that we can influence events by the power of our focused thoughts, the power to co-create consciously with God.

Process theology is often referred to as process-*relational* theology, because it shows not only that we are all interconnected (by the inclusion of all past experiences in us, although we are not consciously aware of much of the past), but also shows how we are all intimately bound up with God in a perpetual collaboration between God and us. Science gives us momentary bursts of lifeless energy; Whitehead adds the God who loves us, leads us, lures us toward greater good, orchestrates events to assist us, and mitigates events that don't turn out well. In each moment, we bring together the pattern of the past, God's perfect possibilities for us, and our power to choose how much of each to include in that moment. God is constantly active in the world, yet God also has a passive, feminine side that preserves all these experiences in the mind of God forever. Process thinker Sallie MacFague proposes viewing God as Mother, Lover, and Friend, in addition to the traditional Father. Suchocki tells us, "Process theology, like all Christian theology, is an attempt to express the wonder of the God who is with us and for us. The categories may be new, drawn from the relational sensitivities of our day, but the story is as old as the gospel."

Chapter Three

The Process and Faith program of the Center for Process Studies, at Claremont, California, which emphasizes "a relational vision of reality," offers the following summary:

The Power of Creation is the Power of Love

Because everything is related;
Because the decision of each event
matters for all events;
Because freedom is a reality;

The greatest power is not coercive force,
but patient, creative, persuading, redeeming,
gracious love. This is God's power,
Which continually works to lure the whole
creation:

To bring enriching diversity and intensity
out of struggle;
To overcome destructive conflict
with greater harmonies;
To redeem the evil wrought in death
and disaster with new life.

The Relational Vision Finds Meaning in Diversity

Process Thought gives a relational vision of reality in which religion and science need not contradict each other, in which one need not devalue other creeds in order to maintain one's own religious heritage, and in which one need not seek to dominate others to find security for oneself. In process thought, meaning, value, and security are given in our relations with others, with God, and with the whole.

Most process thinkers also accept the essence of personalism and panentheism. Process New Thought adds a particular type of practical application of process thought.

Much has been said and written about the power of the mind. Even rip-roaring materialists acknowledge certain epiphenomena that seem to be useful. We hear secularized distortions of New Thought all the time: "Mind over matter." "You have but to picture it, and it is yours." "Use the power of your mind to make others obey you."

This is *not* New Thought, and it never has been. New Thoughters would agree that the mind has power, but like a giant electromagnet, its power to attract is limited. Run an electric current through that magnet, and it's a different story. The magnet alone can lift two pounds; electrified, its capacity is 2,000 pounds. This is similar to the difference between a mind trying to work its own will and a mind centered on God. Two pounds, or two thousand pounds. But any analogy is limited, and this one ends here, for in the first place, the human mind couldn't work at all apart from God, and in the second place, God is not an impersonal force like electricity. The electricity analogy simply helps us understand the nature and power of God a little better than does the old image of an ill-tempered ancient Oriental potentate hurling thunderbolts from a golden throne somewhere in outer space. More about that in a moment.

New Thought principles underlie most American success literature from the mid-nineteenth century onward, but many, if not most, success authors stress the power of the mind with little or no reference to God. Yet God makes the difference. God gives the increase, as St. Paul told the Corinthians (I Cor. 3:6).

Chapter Three

People often say that there's nothing new in New Thought, because it is based on ancient wisdom. But the name *New Thought* can be likened to *metanoia*, "Be ye transformed by the re*new*ing of your mind." (Rom. 12:2) The new thought in New Thought is *yours*, and all your brightest and best new thoughts come from God, the source of all newness. Your not-so-good new thoughts are the result of your choosing too much of the past at the expense of the new possibilities that God gives you.

Which Breed of God Should I Pick?

God? Which one? Whose idea of God should we adopt? Some years ago, Alan noticed that *God* spelled backward was *dog*, and hit on the notion of writing a book about God along the lines of a dog book, a sort of dyslexic guide to the deity, as he put it. (Have you heard about the dyslexic agnostic insomniac? He woke up in the middle of the night wondering whether there was a dog.) The dog book now bears the title *A Guide to the Selection and Care of Your Personal God*. There's a whole divine kennel of canine conceptions to choose from, which we briefly reviewed in our more recent jointly-written book (*New Thought: A Practical American Spirituality*). You probably wouldn't pick the Archaic Terrorer or the Pure-Bred High-Nosed, but many people are attracted to the low-profile World-Woofer, or best of all, the lovable Mixed Breed.

Do we have to choose a conceptualization of God? Isn't it enough just to lead a good life? Can't we just follow the recipe, use natural laws, think happy thoughts, visualize and affirm, be very diligent in our practice, floss after brushing, and forget the theology? There's so much disagreement even among the mainstream Christian churches, let alone among the world's great religions. Who's right? Who knows? Who cares? Just tell us how to get our own sweet way and be happy. Some of the people who do the most for other people in terms of great inventions or charities or medical care or inspiration in the form of art or entertainment don't seem to be religious or God-centered or even spiritual. So why should we bother?

The answer again is in modeling excellent performers, if you want their excellent results. Brother Lawrence believed in a God who was loving and therefore a person. Every one of the New Thought founders was centered on God, and nearly every one of them came from a traditional Christian background. Although they found the theism of traditional Christianity wanting, they clung to the teachings of Jesus. And Jesus, the greatest of all excellent performers for us to model, believed in one God, whom he called Father (actually, the Aramaic word *abba* used in the Gospels means Daddy, and perhaps even Mommy/Daddy, according to our friend, Aramaic scholar and New Thought minister Mary Beth Olson). Jesus told his disciples when they asked him to teach them to pray, that they should begin "Our Father." In other words, we, too, should relate to God as to a loving parent. Some people have not had the experience of knowing a loving father, so they may choose other names, other metaphors.

Too many people still associate the word *God* with the anthropomorphic, male-dominant hierarchical image of the capricious old guy in the sky who had to be placated or pleaded with. Anthropomorphism means attributing human qualities to non-humans such as Peter Rabbit, Mickey Mouse, or even Mike Mulligan's steam shovel, Mary Ann, in the children's classic. If we are being anthropomorphic on purpose and not out of childish ignorance, it can be useful, or at least fun. In the case of God, anthropomorphism often turns up in traditional theism along with the notion of God transcendent, "out there" somewhere, generally inaccessible, just what we would expect from a giant and powerful human being who also has magical powers to spy on little children and see when they are being naughty. On top of that, we have omnipotence, the notion that God has absolutely every bit of power there is. Well, folks, free will, freedom to choose, is a power; and if God has *all* the power, there goes your free will. It's an illusion. You're just a puppet on God's string, or perhaps God grants you the illusion of freedom out of the goodness of God's heart in a sort of cosmic game of Let's Pretend. Obviously, as process philosopher Charles Hartshorne has pointed out, we need to rework our definition of omnipotence.

Most of the mainstream Christian churches no longer buy the ridiculously anthropomorphic notion of traditional theism one hundred percent, if indeed they ever did. People who don't care for this notion of God as tyrant sometimes want to avoid even the name *God*, which they associate with this primitive, outmoded idea, so often part of a toxic religious belief. Many people then turn to the Eastern concept of a god or godhead or emptiness or pure potentiality that is not anthropomorphic and that is immanent, close and available, everywhere. Sounds good, so far. That position holds that we are all one with this god, sometimes referred to as the Ground of All Being, from which we spring like waves from the ocean and into which we eventually melt.

But take a closer look. This god, or whatever it should be called, is not only not anthropomorphic, it has no self-awareness, rationality, or consciously chosen purpose, which are the defining qualities of personhood. Some of those whom Westerners are inclined to call pantheists prefer some other name, since they maintain that the ultimate reality is not a personal God but is something that transcends all categories; the term *neutral monism* sometimes is used. However, for the sake of simplicity we'll use the term *pantheism* to cover a range of views including the idea that nature is awe-inspiring and deserves to be called God, that there is a divine being that includes everything without any distinction of self and other, and the neutral monistic view that there is an utterly indescribable One that is or gives rise to everything. Whatever it is that any of these roughly pantheistic outlooks refers to, it is not a loving parent or a wise partner; it is an it, and an it cannot love. If you have experienced the love of God, then you did not experience this breed of god. And if we examine this model logically, we find that we have no free will, no role to play, no power of choice. We just go round and round on the wheel of death and rebirth, until we finally are released into blessed nothingness. No divine plan for the universe, just illusions, at least as understood in a rational way. Don't desire anything, keep a stiff upper lip, and maybe you will be lucky enough to stay dead when you die. This is a composite, rough-and-ready view of the god of traditional pantheism. Traditional theism holds pantheism to be a heresy, in all its 57 varieties. (Well, would you believe eight?) Both traditional theism and traditional pantheism get modified from time to time as people become aware of their logical deficiencies and try to clean them up a little. And of course, pantheism doesn't think much of theism, much of which is so childish and primitive.

Please note that in no way do we question your right to believe as you please, and your experience is your experience. What we are questioning is the *interpretation*—while seated in the philosopher's armchair—of what may well be an ineffable experience, the struggle to put that experience into words. The philosopher can respect the mystical experience, but must stay within the bounds of reason and logic, or forfeit the greatest gift we as human beings possess.

Pantheism is mostly found in the East; theism mostly in the West. Pointing to the inadequacies of both metaphysical systems is not to say that East and West cannot learn a lot from each other. They can learn from, and even incorporate some

Chapter Three

teachings from each other. They can value the differences between them. Many of the great Christian mystics were seemingly pantheists, or were accused of it. Some forms of pantheism value mystical experience above all else, even above reason. This sounds appealing to some New Thoughters, because of the common mystical experience interpreted as meaning "God is all there is." But to rank mysticism above common sense is the same kind of error that ranked science above religion, to the detriment of both. The eye of reason must mediate between the eye of flesh and the eye of contemplation, to keep things in balance, with no one eye dominating the others. Otherwise, the person who hears the voice of God may turn out like mass murderer Son of Sam, who heard voices telling him to kill people.

Many New Thoughters may find it practically impossible to conceive of New Thought without the pantheistic belief that God literally is everything, that there is nothing but God. However, Horatio W. Dresser, whose parents were among the very first New Thoughters and who was one of the first historians of the movement, did characterize New Thought in non-pantheistic terms, and neatly expressed it as follows:

> The New Thought is a practical philosophy of the inner life in relation to health, happiness, social welfare, and success. Man as a spiritual being is living an essentially spiritual life, for the sake of the soul. His life proceeds from within outward, and makes for harmony, health, freedom, efficiency, service. He needs to realize the spiritual truth of his being, that he may rise above all ills and all obstacles into fullness of power. Every resource he could ask for is at hand, in the omnipresent [as loving guide, not as the totality of oneself] divine wisdom. Every individual can learn to draw upon divine resources. The special methods of New Thought grow

out of this central spiritual principle. Much stress is put upon inner or spiritual concentration and inner control, because each of us needs to become still to learn how to be affirmative, optimistic. Suggestion or affirmation is employed to banish ills and errors and establish spiritual truth in their place. Silent or mental treatment is employed to overcome disease and secure freedom and success. The New Thought then is not a substitute for Christianity, but an inspired return to the original teaching and practice of the gospels. It is not hostile to science but wishes to spiritualize all facts and laws. It encourages each man to begin wherever he is, however conditioned, whatever he may find to occupy his hands; and to learn the great spiritual lessons taught by this present experience.

Oneness often is identified with the idea that we are one with God in the sense that there is nothing of us that is not God. However, Dresser affirmed the oneness in a different sense, without embracing pantheism:

> The essence of the New Thought, as I understand it, is the *oneness of life*; the great truth, namely, that all things work together toward a high ideal in the kingdom of the Spirit. Otherwise stated, it is the truth that God lives with us, in every moment of existence, in every experience, every sorrow and every struggle.

Dresser attacked the belief that "man is 'divine,'" that God is "the sole Reality 'in' the self." He affirmed that "Man then is not 'one with God,' but . . . may be led into unison or conjunction with the Lord . . . . by the operation of the Divine love and wisdom through [not as] us . . ."

Chapter Three

Some "theologies" prefer to be known as *nontheistic*, because although they view nature as sacred they do not believe in any god, just a sort of godhead or source. Because their "god"—or lack of one—is roughly identified with the world rather than differentiated or even separated from it, scholars classify them as pantheists. And so the two main views of God are polar opposites. Thesis, antithesis. Mexican standoff. We'll return to this thrilling duel a little later.

Jesus

Meanwhile, back at the ranch, New Thought leaders, free thinkers all, abandoned much of the superstition of traditional Christianity, but retained allegiance to the teachings of the central figure of Christianity, Jesus, and to the God that Jesus believed in and trusted. Why? Why not just worship the power of the mind, love nature, lead a good life, and forget this God business? Why single out this one human being as a special example for all of us to follow?

This is not the place to go into the details of the evidence that Jesus in fact rose from the dead and appeared to numerous eyewitnesses on several occasions, nor the place to go into the extensive support for these accounts by scholars from disciplines ranging from forensic medicine to anthropology to the arts. The resurrection appearances were necessary to demonstrate that Jesus had mastered death as well as life; however, our attention needs to focus on the events that took place during his earthly life.

Before his death, this human being named Jesus was healing the sick, raising the dead, and demonstrating abundance, all the while teaching his followers to love one another and to love God, who, he said, loved them—and us—like a father. This human being was unquestionably God-centered, and taught his followers to be the same. Many thoughtful people consider this man to be unique. Yet what he achieved is worthless to us unless we can imitate him, and he said that we could and would; "He who believes in Me, the works that I do he will do also; and greater works than these he will do" (John 14:12). He was human, just like us—*and divine, just like us!* We, too, contain that Christ mind, that spark of the divine, that initial aim, those perfect possibilities from God. Jesus was able to show us the way to contact and use that divine power. He may have been a lot farther along the path than any of us, but we can walk that same path.

In our culture, *Lord* and *Master* are no longer useful titles, but we can see Jesus as our way-shower, our elder brother, since he told us that we are all children of the same loving, heavenly Father, to whom he cried out while he was dying in agony on the cross. This relationship to God as his parent was therefore genuine and deep, not just a teaching device for his disciples. Moreover, he demonstrated how we can have an adult relationship in partnership with that same Mother/Father God.

Jesus accepted God's initial aims, God's perfect possibilities for him, more than anyone else before or since. For this reason, he deserves the title *Christ*. The Christ, the Greek equivalent of the Hebrew Messiah, as the annointed ruler was expected to free his people. We, too, can earn that title and become the liberators of our lives, the rulers of our consciousness, by accepting God's initial aim, synonymous with the mind of Christ, which St. Paul tells us we have (1 Cor. 2:16). Jesus, then, was unique in degree, but not in kind. Perhaps he had worked to develop his high degree of spirituality in many earlier lifetimes. Maybe, as some have suggested, he was a reincarnation of Moses, Elijah, or even the Buddha. In process terms, he helped in significant degree to free us from the heavy burden of the past by his life and teachings, thereby making it easier for us to accept the offers of

Chapter Three

God that liberate us into fuller living. Making it easier was done by his increasing the positive content of our past, thereby reducing the contrast between our past and the divine possibilities.

Not all process thinkers are Christians, and process thought is applicable in any religion as well as outside of religion. However, for process thinkers who follow the teachings of Jesus, he is the central focus of the activity of God in history. Suchocki elaborates:

> God works with the world as it is to guide it toward what it might be. This means that God's own nature influences the world in every developing moment. Insofar as the world responds positively to this influence, the world will be living according to the reign of God in history. In this sense, process theology is most compatible with the biblical portrayal that Jesus is the realized presence of God's reign in history, for the process understanding of the incarnation is that Jesus responds positively to God's influence in each moment of his life. In Jesus, therefore, God's reign is already present.

Although we may include wisdom from numerous religious traditions, New Thoughters in putting together their own individual religious beliefs usually turn to the teachings of Jesus of Nazareth, the only human being to conquer death. Traditional Christianity may have encumbered the simple teachings of an itinerant first-century rabbi with a bunch of dogma that we may or may not choose to go along with, but the basic message is about love, unconditional love, overflowing from the Father in us, through us to our neighbor. And that message includes joy, peace, and abundance. W. R. Inge, Dean of St. Paul's Cathedral in London early in this century, stated it beautifully when he wrote in his *Outspoken Essays*, "The voice of God within speaks in the tones of Jesus of Nazareth" (p. 54).

The God that Jesus called Father is not off in space somewhere, but within. He is patient, loving, forgiving, and always listening when called upon. He wants good things for his children. We know all this from the words of Jesus as reported in the Gospels. Although we may not have absolute proof of the truth of any single part of them, they are worth betting our life on. See how believing them works in your life.

Well, fine, some nice guy who did a lot of good and still got himself killed came back from the dead. Let's do what the man said, since he obviously had a line on how to live happily and well. We find that impressive, and we do not choose to follow science to the exclusion of religion, for we see that there is much that science simply cannot deal with. We may or may not choose to follow one of the denominations that has sprung up around Jesus in the religion that is known as Christianity, or even some of the newer sects that follow Jesus but do not label themselves Christian. What are our choices if we want some understanding of a God who really is "a very present help in trouble" (Ps. 46)? Isn't there any sort of consensus among religions, some core beliefs about what is real and dependable?

This is where things start to get complicated. Up until the last century, Christianity was a kind of package deal wherein you had to buy into traditional theism if you wanted to be a Christian. It didn't occur to anybody to simply read what Jesus said and try to live by it without buying all the stuff about Jesus handed down by the ecclesiastical hierarchy. And it was pretty bad stuff, by today's standards. The church was at war with science, not to mention common sense. The Reformation may have helped a little, but mostly replaced one set of crazy notions with another. Clear thinkers were repelled: how could any clear thinker in modern times accept such strange superstitions and obviously manmade notions? And Jews and Muslims were not given the truth about Jesus and his teachings—small wonder, but sad, for the basic gospel of love is not at all at odds with the teachings of those religions. But they, too, have their share of strange superstitions and manmade notions. Traditional theism just doesn't cut it in the modern—not to mention postmodern—world.

Meanwhile, people in the Eastern religions probably never even heard of Jesus, or dismissed what they heard as wild and distorted rumors. The god that they were taught about was usually the god of pantheism, who did not capriciously hurl thunderbolts, but might as well not exist at all for all the good it—not he or she—did. The god of pantheism is everywhere present, and we are all part of it, and eventually melt back into it, for pantheism holds that we have no permanent individual identity. It's not surprising that traditional Christianity, built around Jesus's idea of asking the Father for help of all kinds, and around his promise of everlasting life (e.g., John 3:16, 6:47) to his followers, regards pantheism as a heresy. Still, many people might regard it as an improvement over traditional theism to have an everywhere-present impersonal god as a sort of force holding things together.

Back to the showdown at the divine kennel. As modernity has started to slide into what for lack of a better name is known in a burst of originality as postmodernity, numerous individuals who did not care to make science their religion have sought to find some spiritual commonality. Perhaps the best known of these was Aldous Huxley, whose perennial philosophy was an attempt to find a common core of truth at the mystical heart of all religions. Unfortunately, although we love mysticism and mystics, what the perennial philosophy turns out to be is pantheism. Oops, out of the frying pan into the fire. Sorry, but that is no improvement over traditional theism, just a different set of problems, mainly involving a lack of logic. And if you are trying to find a common core in all religions, you don't begin by throwing out the major portions of Christianity, Judaism, and Islam, all part of traditional theism and all regarding pantheism as heresy. Not a promising beginning at all. And you can't just do what many in ancient Rome wanted the early Christians to do, and just set up another altar to the Christian god next to the altars of the pagan deities, so we can all worship everybody's gods and we'll all get along. That would not have been a win for the Christians, and if you can't have win/win, sometimes there has to be no deal. Alas, many New Thoughters, in extricating themselves from the errors of Christianity, fell into the snare of perennialism. They just didn't realize that there is another possibility.

Chapter Three

The Arrival of the Cavalry, German Style

In nineteenth-century Germany, a philosopher named Carl Friedrich Wilhelm Krause sought to synthesize traditional theism and pantheism into something higher than either one, yet acceptable to both. Thesis, antithesis, synthesis, for all you St. Louis Hegelians. Krause came up with something for which he coined the word *panentheism*. According to Arnulf Zweig, writing in *The Encyclopedia of Philosophy*, Krause's writings are extremely difficult to read and loaded with neologisms, German nouns that you can't even translate into German! But he seems to have gotten the job done. His work was embraced around the turn of the century by the aforementioned Dean Inge of St. Paul's, author of *Personal Idealism and Mysticism*. You say you're New Age and you want somebody more up to date? According to Marilyn Ferguson, author of *The Aquarian Conspiracy*, the father of New Age is Jesuit priest and paleontologist Teilhard de Chardin, who did not use the term *panentheism*, but whose work is classified as such.

Panentheism is not exactly a household word, though we're working on it. What is panentheism? If pantheism says that God is everywhere, panentheism says that everywhere is in God. "In him we live and move and have our being" (Acts 17:28). It says that the universe is God's body. Hartshorne elaborates:

> God is not simply the world-whole of stars, planets, and smaller or larger groupings, but . . . a supreme and all-embracing *experiencing* of the whole. . . . Plato says, and in this shows his greatness, that the divine Soul includes the divine body, not vice versa. He does not explain, but my reason is simple: subjects include their objects.

The Presence of God

We are one with God in the sense of our interconnectedness and our identifying (in the psychological sense) with God, *yet we retain our individuality*, which is necessary in order for us to have free will. If we are not distinguishable from God, our free will is an illusion. We are a one that is made up of many. E pluribus unum (haven't you heard that somewhere before?), not a monolithic oneness. California may some day fall into the ocean, but it's not going to melt into Massachusetts or Maryland or Montana. They retain their individuality, even though they are interconnected in many ways and work together in many ways.

If we understand the nature of any experience (which is what we ought to mean by mind or spirit), we will see that it is impossible for God (or whatever you consider ultimate) to be everything. All experiences, including God, feel (include) all earlier experiences, but it makes no sense to claim that anything can be anything other than its unique self, with its unique perspective on everything.

Personalist philosophers hold that personality is the ultimate explanatory principle. Panentheists—along with the personalist philosophers—say that God is the ultimate person: not the ultimate human being, but a self-conscious being having both masculine and feminine qualities, as do we. That is not the same as saying that God is a man or a woman. God is without gender. Emmet Fox notes,

> A great practical difficulty in discussing God is the fact that we have no suitable pronoun to employ. We have to use the words "he" and "him." We have no alternative, but these words are very misleading because they inevitably suggest a man or male animal. To say "she" and "her" would be equally absurd, and the word "it," besides seeming to lack in reverence, suggests an inanimate and unintelligent object.

Chapter Three

The point is that God as person is a being to whom we can relate, not as slaves to a tyrant, and not—once we have arrived at adulthood—as children. We need to think in terms of *inter*dependent relationships, in which men and women are equal partners, and in which God is senior partner and we are junior partners. We have already mentioned Stephen Covey's maturity continuum that goes from dependence to independence to interdependence, the highest form of maturity. We cannot be interdependent without first becoming independent, fully differentiated, fully other. We are other than God, though we are never separate from God. This is a vital distinction, because it takes two to tango, and to love. We can be made in the image of God as a child is the spit and image of its parent, but that does not mean that we are identical with God.

The God of panentheism transcends all of us, as did the God of traditional theism. This allows for wonders we can't even begin to imagine. The God of panentheism is also immanent. "Closer is he than breathing, nearer than hands and feet," wrote Alfred, Lord Tennyson in *A Higher Pantheism*. The name *higher pantheism* can be used to refer to panentheism, which corrects the philosophical mistakes in pantheism while retaining what is valuable. In panentheism coupled with process thought (as it generally is), God's character is utterly reliable and unchanging, yet because we are part of God's body, God to that extent changes and grows as we grow. The God of panentheism is everywhere present and available, impartial, and dependable. We look to God as the ultimate, the source of our basic principles, or our rules of conduct. We say that this is a universe of law; it operates in accordance with relatively fixed patterns, so it is predictable. A law is a description of how things habitually work, as in "What goes up must come down."

God: Up Close and Personal

We must be careful not to confuse *person*, *personal*, and *personality*. A person may or may not be a human being. Animals certainly have emotions, and can be purposive, but very few animals are self-aware, and even fewer are likely to be rational. A person is self-aware, consciously purposive, and rational. Dolphins may turn out to be persons. If there are angels, they are persons. And God is the ultimate person, meaning that God is personal, or has personhood. If God lacks personhood, we have a situation in which the creature is more advanced than the creator. *Personal* does not mean in philosophy what it means in common parlance: something for one's private use, such as a monogram, or a diary. Nor does it correspond to traditional religious use, such as the expression "my personal Savior." Nor does it mean a lesser appearance of one's underlying self.

God has the positive aspects of personality, but not its limitations. God is not prejudiced or angry or lazy. God's personality is utterly loving, dependable, wise, honest, and impartial. Sadly, some New Thoughters refer to God as "It," a cold, impersonal term that does not acknowledge the personhood, let alone the love, of God.

We keep remembering the story about the little girl who was afraid of being left alone in the dark, and her mother told her not to worry, because God was there. "But I want a God with skin on," was the reply. She wanted a personal God, one she could relate to, one who seemed real to her, not some kind of abstraction. Some Christian writers say that we view God through a Christ-shaped keyhole. Jesus did indeed relate to God as personal, and taught us to do so, too.

Chapter Three

God's Mind and God's Body

God has a mind, and so do we. More precisely, God is a mind, and so are we. Our minds, like our bodies, are in God and connected with God. At the same time, we are individuals with free will, distinct from God. We are all within one divine mind, and that one mind includes many minds, interconnected. There is a grove of trees somewhere in the western United States in which the roots have become so intertwined that the trees actually make up a single organism. Arthur Koestler, without adding a new idea, coined the term *holon* to describe something made up of lesser somethings. Using that terminology, God's body is the ultimate holon, yet God is more than merely the sum of the parts. Philosophers tend to distrust metaphor in their work, but once in a while, metaphor is the only way of getting at something that is difficult to express, such as the nature of our relationship with God. There is no getting away from God, yet God can do nothing without us. So God and we are a cocreative team.

What kind of world is this, this body of God? Clearly, it is not material, but mental, and matter is a collection of contemporaneously existing minds. The world is in God, and there is nothing outside of God. And the world is not static, but dynamic, constantly changing. The Greek philosopher Heraclitus had it right when he pointed out that you can't step into the same river twice, yet the world is far more dynamic than even Heraclitus realized. At this point, we turn to the quantum physicists, who tell us that even what seems so solid is anything but, that it's full of space and tiny subatomic particles that whirl and shimmer and sing. Remember that Whitehead tells us that all this activity in nature is *alive*, new every moment, and that newness can only come from God.

The Presence of God

All our big, beautiful, exciting, daring ideas come from God. God is the great initiator. Our job is to finish what God starts, and of course, God has things all lined up waiting to help us, other things that God initiates. God is eager for us to receive our highest good, but God never forces us. We are free to say no to God. Of course, we then take the consequences, and we learn the necessary lessons. God is quite willing for us to have whatever experiences we need in order to learn what we need to learn, but God does have preferences, and those preferences are always for our highest good. God wants what is really best for us, and revises that best, moment by moment, to take into account what has happened. What is best now, what is best at the next now, and the next?

What is usually best is to be proactive, as Covey's Habit One indicates, to take responsibility for what happens next, rather than trying to change the past. We all have free will, the ability to choose at each moment. We may also be influenced by other people and events, but that is still our choice.

Changing the Pattern of the Past

The good news from process thought, and especially Process New Thought, is that we can change our lives, one experience at a time. These increasingly positive experiences pile up and form a new pattern of the past as a background behind us. As we gradually create closer and closer approximations of what we want our lives to be like, the difference between the pattern of the past and where we would like to be grows less and less. The trick to changing the pattern of the past is to work in the present, which immediately becomes the past. Hence, it becomes easier and easier to choose God's perfect plan, as the contrast between it and the past decreases.

Chapter Three

Have you ever been to a fast food place where there are huge nets filled with styrofoam balls of different bright colors, for children to climb into and play with? Imagine that you are standing in front of a huge pile of those balls, each one representing an experience. You decide that you would like your background to be red, so you begin to choose red balls, one at a time, and throw them back over your shoulder. Gradually, your background gets redder and redder, unless you suddenly switch to selecting blue balls, or a sign descends from heaven reading "Green is a popular color this year," and you change your mind. And all the time, God is helping you, holding out perfect possibilities ("There's a red ball right over there"; "Look over to your left"). And if you sin and grab the wrong color, or your aim is off, God does not judge or condemn. The sign descending from heaven never reads, "YOU IDIOT!" But you are still subject to the laws of the universe: God can't just turn off the law of gravity so that your balls/experiences will pile up faster, or pour red or green paint from heaven to color all your balls at once. So we have this exquisite balance of love and law. Law, an abstraction, cannot act. Laws merely describe the way that experiences habitually act.

The pattern of the past that you are trying to create might be wellness, or financial prosperity, or a better relationship. You create it one thought at a time, one experience at a time. And you exist one experience at a time; you really are a new person many times per second.

God has infinite patience, and God will let you do whatever you wish. You must take the consequences of your actions, but even there, God is at work mitigating evil. Once you have learned your lesson, there is no "bad karma" haunting you, just the consequences of your previous actions. The wonderful, unmerited gift of God's grace is being offered to you every moment, but even grace is not forced upon you; you must choose to accept or reject it, just as you must choose to accept or reject any of God's perfect possibilities for you. "The presence of God in us is divine grace," observe process theologians John Cobb and David Griffin in their book, *Process Theology*. "Peace . . . is an alignment of ourselves with God's grace." And, a little later, "There is both divine grace and human responsibility. Christian action entails both." There is that cocreation again, that joining of ourselves with God in each occasion of experience. In our first book, Alan expressed it as a formula: Past + Divine Possibilities + Choice = Cocreation.

Hell, and Other Graceless States

Although God is everywhere present and available to us, we can choose to effectively shut God out of our lives, for God will not violate our free will; indeed, God cannot, for that would be against God's loving nature, as well as the way that reality simply is. There are some things that just can't be otherwise; this is one of them. It's the kind of thing that metaphysics seeks to discover.

When we shut God out, in our ignorance or despair, we call that state of consciousness *hell*. But as Emmet Fox put it, the gates of hell are swinging doors. Because we put ourselves in, we can also get ourselves out again, simply by turning to God. And even if one believes that one can't believe in God because to believe in God would create a duality, God is right there, loving, luring toward greater good, and offering perfect possibilities. God does what it is God's nature to do, and goes right on doing it, whether or not you believe in God.

To be an atheist and remain one is to be stuck in an adolescent stage of spiritual growth. It is a sign of healthy growth to question beliefs that one previously inherited from others and swallowed without question, and it only becomes a problem if one stays in that skeptical frame of mind. Jettisoning childish, outmoded, inadequate images of God is progress. As one New Thoughter observed to atheist Madalyn Murray O'Hair, "Tell me about the god you don't believe in and I probably don't believe in him, either." Healthy adult curiosity wants to learn more about God. As one scientist put it, "We agree that God created the world; now we're trying to find out how he did it." Process thinkers would say that God always has been cocreating the world.

A myth is an approximation of truth, a story told to make a point, not to record exact details of history. Many myths bear scant resemblance to reality, but still have value because of what they teach. Theologian Paul Tillich referred to myths that we realize are not literal truths as *broken*. Unbroken myths are those that people hold without realizing that they are myths. Broken myths may still be useful, as is the notion of Santa Claus. Many old notions about God are broken or unbroken myths.

One common problem in scientific research is to design a study in such a way that one cuts off the possibility of seeing what is really there. This happens frequently with respect to intangibles, things that are difficult to measure; and it provides grist for the skeptic's mill. One of Whitehead's contributions to Western thought was his Fallacy of Misplaced Concreteness, which consists of one's mistaking an abstraction for something concrete. An abstraction in this sense is a collection of living experiences, but it is not itself alive. All too often, skeptics try to reduce God to an abstraction in the usual sense, and then fault it for being limited, which is one of the dangers of viewing God as impersonal. God is indeed impartial, "no respecter of persons" (Acts 10:34), but God is no mere abstraction, in either sense.

Open at the Top

Poor philosophers! They get insults from all directions. Even Ernest Holmes labeled philosophy as "opinion," which can be interpreted as both insulting to philosophy and inaccurate. Philosophy is required to go by rules, the logical rules of reasoning, just as do the sciences that evolved from it. Any philosophical statement is subject to criticism. The onlooker is the judge of who won the debate by the strength of the argument or the criticism of it. Any mere opinion comes from the bystander, not from the philosopher. Of course, we are not talking about cracker barrel philosophy, which is indeed opinion, and probably not based on much evidence. What really matters in a philosophical argument is its internal consistency. Reality goes right on being reality, in any case.

Holmes on occasion defended himself ably against the charge of pantheism, showing that he was aware of its limitations, yet on other occasions, he fell into it. In following Thomas Troward, a prominent early New Thought writer, Holmes got himself into difficulties by trying to reify ("thingify") law, an example of the Fallacy of Misplaced Concreteness. Yet Holmes was a superb practitioner with his systematized Spiritual Mind Treatment, understanding the necessity for being absolutely solid and unwavering in one's faith in God during treatment. And it was Holmes who said that New Thought—or his version of it, Religious Science—should be "open at the top," meaning open-minded, ready to accept correction as better data or better reasoning become available. Were he still alive, we like to believe that it would be possible to sit down and discuss these matters with him and have him agree that process thought, panentheism, and personalism (which he almost certainly must have heard of in the course of his friendship with personalist philosopher Ralph Tyler Flewelling) are the direction in which New Thought should be heading in the twenty-first century. Similarly, Unity co-founder Charles Fillmore reserved the right to change his mind at any time on any subject, and we believe that he, too, with his unlimited curiosity about science, would also have seen the beauty and power of process thought and panentheism.

Study vs. Treatment

Emmet Fox notes,

> Studying metaphysics is one thing, but treatment is quite another. The rules for one cannot be applied to the other if success is to be attained. People often confuse these two things and consequently fail to demonstrate. When you are studying—reading a metaphysical book, listening to a lecture, or thinking over the Truth that you know—you should be open-minded, wisely critical, being as analytical as you please. . . .
>
> When you are treating, the exact opposite policy is the right one. Then you must be dogmatic, insistent, arbitrary, cocksure, and mentally closed to anything but the Truth about the problem. . . . you can use your mental power for learning more Truth, or you can use it for applying the Truth you already possess; but these processes are still two different things.

Many people in New Thought strive to be solid and unwavering all the time, not just during treatments. In this way, they get stuck in inconsistencies and contradictions. It's one thing for a mystic to have an overwhelming experience and declare, "We are all one." In psychology, universal oneness is the highest order of perception. It's another thing to distinguish ineffable experience from interpretation of it following so quickly that it may be confused with the mystical experience.

And it is something else altogether to take such a vague statement and build a philosophy around it. What kind of one? How many is one? People in New Thought like to say, "There is nothing but God" or "God is all there is," or "I am God," recognizing this sense of oneness with God. Such statements are wonderful as a part of a treatment. But if it is literally true that we are one hundred percent identical with God, then we have no free will, or it is an illusion. This view makes God celestial Play-Doh, shaping itself into you and us.

Another issue is the difference between *other* and *separate*. We are not God, in that we are *other than* God, and yet *we are never separate from God*. God is indeed everywhere present as loving influence. We are one with God the same way that the United States of America is one nation, a one made up of many. It is not a monolithic oneness (philosophers call that *quan*titative monism). On the other hand, God and we are of the same (one) nature: mind, or spirit (philosophers call that *qual*itative monism). All of us independent thinkers, together with the mini-minds that compose the rest of nature, make up the body of God. Since God's body is in God's mind, we are in the mind of God. However, you are not your body, and God is not God's body. We are not indistinguishable from God. This is absolutely vital in order for us to have real free will rather than some illusion of freedom that is really God pulling our strings. "I am one with God" or "Ye are gods, and all of you are children of the most High" (Ps. 82:6) means that we are of the same nature as God, made in God's image and likeness, just as we are the same nature as our parents, flesh of their flesh, and so we say we are one family, one with our father and mother. Jesus said, "I and My Father are one" (John 10:30), "I am in the Father, and the Father in Me" (John 14:10), and "My Father is greater than I" (John 14:28). This makes it pretty clear. There is a huge difference between being *in* God and being God.

The relationship of ourselves and God is similar to that of ourselves and our bodies. Hartshorne says:

> The open secret of the mind-body relation is this: *our cells respond to our feelings (and thoughts) because we respond to their feelings* (and would respond to their thoughts if they had any). Hurt my cells and you hurt me. Give my cells a healthy life, and they give me a feeling of vitality and at least minimal happiness. My sense of welfare tends to sum up theirs, and their misfortunes tend to become negative feelings of mine. I feel what many cells feel, integrating these feelings into a higher unity. I am somewhat as their deity, their fond heavenly companion. They gain their direction and sense of the goodness of life partly from intuiting my sense of that goodness, which *takes theirs intuitively into account.*

Portrait— er, Movie of God, New Every Moment

Summing all this up, what sort of portrait of God do we emerge with? A portrait that is constantly changing as the universe changes. Whitehead calls God "the poet of the world, with tender patience leading it by his vision of truth, beauty, and goodness," and "the great companion, the fellow sufferer who understands." He describes God as luring us, never coercing us. The Bible in the book of Revelation refers to God as "Alpha and Omega, the beginning and the ending" (1:8), and in Hebrews as "the author and finisher of our faith" (12:2). Process thought says that God initiates everything, and then lovingly preserves each experience after its moment of development. God is both active (masculine), and passive (feminine), though God, as we have already discussed, has no gender.

The Presence of God

God is everywhere present and available, as omnipotent as it is possible for any being to be without negating the free will of all the other beings, and as omniscient as it is possible to be: since the future hasn't happened yet, God can know only the probabilities. God's loving, dependable character never changes even though God is growing as we grow. God is the source of all our best and most beautiful ideas, of all newness in the world. We can relate to God as the ultimate person.

God is always there for us no matter how badly we mess up, still loving us unconditionally. Yet at the same time, the orderliness of the universe is such that we receive the consequences of our actions. We are responsible for our lives, and the more we can assume responsibility, the happier we will be. God knows this, for God knows all there is to know, and God wants the highest good for us. God never "sends" sickness or suffering. God never "calls someone home." We couldn't ask for a better senior partner in any undertaking. God and we are truly interdependent, needing each other.

What About God's Body?

It is impossible for science to go back before the Big Bang, but philosophers can speculate on what may have been then. Not only has God always been, but God has always had a body. There was no original, unilateral, by God only, creation; God always has co-created with something already in existence. It may have looked quite different at different times, such as before the Big Bang, yet it has always been there. So there has always been something or someone to say yes or no to God's perfect possibilities.

We're all part of each other's environment, part of the background from which each occasion of experience develops, so we are all interconnected. Whitehead says, "Each task of

Chapter Three

creation is a social effort, employing the whole universe. Each novel actuality is a new partner adding a new condition. Every new condition can be absorbed into additional fullness of attainment."

We're all parts of the same system, so what affects one affects all, at least a little. This means that it doesn't make sense for us to despoil our planet, or any other planet, for that matter. It means that although this is an abundant universe, we can create artificial shortages by hoarding or by improper distribution, so we need to use our common sense and show courtesy and consideration to each other. As the most complex creatures to evolve that we know of, human beings have dominion over other creatures (Genesis 1:28), but as Stephen Covey explains, you won't have golden eggs for very long if you neglect the goose that lays them. Covey refers to this principle as paying attention to both production and production capability. Adam was supposed to "tend and keep" the Garden of Eden, even though he was free to enjoy the fruits and plants that grew there.

It's ironic, really, that the royal road to freedom is to assume greater responsibility for ourselves and the world around us. It is not leaving things to government, the churches, or other charities; rather, it is taking effective control of our own lives. St. Augustine said that we should love God and do as we please, in that order. To love someone includes loving and respecting that person's body (the subpersonal groupie-like minds serving the personal mind that is the person). Since the universe is God's body, we are committed to loving everyone and everything. Love, of course, means goodwill, wishing someone or something well. It doesn't mean you have to like everyone or everything equally; it just means that once the goodwill is in place, along with taking responsibility for tending our "garden," the sky's the limit in terms of setting goals and achieving them, succeeding in whatever one sets out to do. You see, part of God's wanting the highest and best for each of us is wanting each of us to be all that we can be, to optimize our greatest talents, our greatest joys and pleasures. This means God wants the fewest wars and the least suffering for everyone, too. It really is a wonderful world, once we get the hang of living in it.

Chapter Three

4. Practical Purposes

How do we apply our practice of the Presence of God to specific ways of building health, wealth, and happiness? Having taken advantage of the learning gained through scientific research to bring our thought processes under control, and having gotten very clear in our thinking about God and our relationship with God, it's time to turn to the task of fulfilling our life's mission and handling whatever challenges may arise along the path.

We know that we are blessed with a loving God in an abundant universe, and we therefore have the right to expect the best of everything for ourselves and for everyone else as well. More than any other religion or spirituality now or at any other time, New Thought concerns itself with the best way to go about the practical application of our power as cocreators with God. Instead of simple worship of God "above" while we continue to struggle "below," this is the quiet, confident expectation that all that the Father has is ours, and that God is down and dirty, right in the fray with us, "the fellow sufferer who understands."

Ernest Holmes, founder of the Religious Science brand of New Thought, is perhaps most famous for his slogan, "There's a power for good in the universe, and you can use it." That power is, of course, the power of God. How do we best use the power of God? Through what has come to be known as Spiritual Mind Treatment, or, for those who prefer a treat instead of a treatment, affirmative prayer. If prayer is communication with God, affirmative prayer is communication with a particular need in mind, something we want to ask for God's help with, for Jesus told us, "Ask, and it shall be given unto you" (Matt. 7:7). We do our asking in a particular way and a particular frame of mind.

We like to think of affirmative prayer as unfolding in three phases, almost like three acts of a drama. Some people make five steps out of it, but we can never remember them, so we keep it simple. You can easily expand our three phases into five steps, if you like.

If you have occasion to think of using the power of God, rather than simply basking in the light of God's presence, or giving intellectual assent to the idea of God's power, then you probably are presently experiencing some problem or difficulty. Maybe you have an illness, or someone you love has a financial need, or you have a relationship difficulty. Whatever it is, your attention is on the problem, not on the solution, and we know from research in psychology that what you give your attention to grows.

Some of traditional Christianity might be horrified at the idea of *using* God or God's power, even to solve pressing problems. The answer to the objection that we shouldn't use God is that we can't avoid doing so. The deeper understanding as to how we can't avoid doing so is found in the structure of all experience. God offers the best possibilities to each experience. To accept those divine suggestions is to use God; to reject them is to abuse God, to go contrary to God's wishes. The alternative explanation—that God is everything, so we can't avoid using God—is decidedly defective, for reasons we have outlined in the last chapter. So when we say we want to use God, we do not mean to try to take unfair advantage of God—as if we ever could—but rather, to turn to God as the ultimate resource, knowing that we can rely on God utterly. But you have already read chapter three, so you know all about that.

If we are going to unite science and religion, as Holmes and others in New Thought set out to do, we must apply a methodical, scientific approach to God, which is to say, collect as much information as possible. If science is a part of the world, it is a part of God's body. If all good ideas come from God, that includes our scientific learnings. One aspect of God is intelligence, so wherever you see intelligence, you are seeing something of God.

Let's review a bit of what we have discovered about God. We have learned that God is good, loving, and everywhere present and available, for everywhere is in God. This means that God is immanent, here within each one of us; as well as transcendent, available everywhere else, too; uniting us all in a complex unity made up of many. Well, it's pretty hard to relate to the idea of a complex unity, and we don't need to try, because Jesus taught us to relate to God as to a loving father. God is personal; in fact, God is the ultimate person without the limitations of human personality. We know that God cares for us and loves us no matter what we do. Furthermore, based on what we have learned from quantum physics and process philosophy, we know that God offers us perfect possibilities, new every moment, divinely calculated to bring us the highest good out of whatever choices we have made in the past, as well as all else that confronts us.

Unfortunately, we are not always ready to accept those perfect possibilities. We cling to the imperfect patterns of the past, to our old beliefs and habits, and we get less-than-perfect results. This is because our attention is on the problem. We need to get our attention onto God, to become realigned with God so that we can say yes to God's perfect possibilities for us, sometimes called *initial aim*, sometimes called the Christ mind. Wayne Dyer likens this to having an FM station drift on your radio, and having to tune it in again. That station is there all the time, but we aren't always tuned in to it. So by realigning ourselves with God, we are getting *in tune with the Infinite*. Hmmm, that would make a great title for a book; in fact, it already has, by Ralph Waldo Trine, a great New Thought author from around the turn of the century.

Affirmative Prayer

Phase One or Act One of affirmative prayer, then, is to get ourselves aligned with God. We do this by turning our attention to God, and the way to do that is "in returning and rest . . . in quietness and in confidence," as Isaiah tells us (30:15). Here science, in the form of research in psychology, comes in with the information that synchronizing the activity of our brain hemispheres gives us optimum creativity and reduces the harmful effects of stress. This synchronization of hemispheres happens at the brain wave frequency called alpha, the state we go through when we're falling asleep or just waking up. Our consciousness consists of four types of brain wave frequency: beta, alpha, theta, and delta; and when alpha dominates the picture, we say we are *in* alpha. Alpha's a very peaceful, calm state used in meditation for thousands of years, and it's reached at will, with a little practice, by *relaxing the body* and closing the eyes so that attention goes inward. Alpha is a higher frequency than theta, in which you're pretty zonked and may have little memory of what happens. Delta is the lowest frequency, and when your brain waves are all delta, you are in the arms of Morpheus, catching a few z's. The highest frequency is beta, or ordinary waking consciousness, in which you are on guard against threats, your cerebral cortex is going crazy with activity, and there's just no channel for you to notice that God is coming through. Of course, God is available any time and everywhere, but some ways of tuning in to God are easier than others. José Silva's Silva Mind Control Method is another example of the use of the power of the alpha state, and Silva is also very God-centered.

Despite how it sometimes feels, our beliefs determine our experiences, not the other way around. This is because our beliefs determine our expectancies, and we generally get what we expect. However, most of our beliefs are unconsciously held,

Practical Purposes

so we may be getting jerked around by some childish, outworn notion that we would not now accept if we were aware of it. Fortunately, we can overwrite these obsolete beliefs by installing new, more useful beliefs and conscientiously looking around for massive support for them.

In the peaceful, powerful, synchronized-hemisphere state of alpha, we can access our other-than-conscious mind. In this alpha state, it is easier to install new, helpful beliefs and remove old, undesirable ones. So the first thing we have to do is get into that alpha state in which we can really feel, and concentrate our attention on, the Presence of God. When we do this successfully, we are aware of our interconnectedness with God, that we are in God and God is in us. Call it meditation, as Ernest Holmes did; or call it going into the silence, as Charles Fillmore did; or call it George, and let George do it; it's getting aligned with God and it's our Phase One.

Phase Two of our mental treatment comes after we have achieved the quiet-mind-aligned-with-God state of Phase One. Phase Two is getting very clear about what we want and claiming it by asking for it specifically, as Jesus taught. We hold still and listen a while for God's input, then we visualize the solving or dissolving of our problem: the illness healed, the limb sound, the bill paid, the face smiling. We don't concern ourselves with *how it will happen*; that's God's part in this process of cocreation. If we get too concerned with the details, that is called *outlining*, and it is limiting. We must be sure to leave God some wiggle room, some opportunity for creativity, because God sees farther than we do.

Although we are all capable of seeing, hearing, or feeling kinesthetically in our imagination, we generally develop a preference or bias for using one of these modes much more than the others, and it doesn't matter which we use. We can use our imagination to paint pictures, or run movies on the backs of our eyelids; or hear voices saying "Congratulations!" or "Wow!"; or just feel what we would feel once the difficulty is ended. And we keep doing it, keep adding details, until it seems real to us and any doubts are dissolved. We may speak or write our description of a successful outcome *as if it had already happened.* However, this may pull us out of the alpha state; so we may wish to save our speaking aloud or writing until later. And we repeat this visualization every time we give ourselves the treatment, until what we want appears in the outside world as well as in the model of the world that we carry in our minds.

It's a good idea to include a qualifier, "this or something better," for we may not always know what is for our highest good, but God does, and God knows what others need, too, and frequently works things out so that several people get what they want at the same time. We happen to think that this is one way that God gets his jollies, working out the timing on people's requests and giving people the plans for what they *really* want rather than just what they think they want, but that may just be our anthropomorphizing. Still, it's way ahead of believing that you have to beg and plead and wheedle and coax and cajole God in an effort to get what you want. Actually, all of this works in a very orderly way that you might describe as lawful. We have already warned you not to go to the other extreme and "thingify" law, as if it were a mechanical sort of semi-android who did your bidding like Lurch, the Frankenstein monster-type butler on the old Addams Family TV show, uuuhhh. We're cocreating *with* God, remember, and as Emmet Fox used to say, the Lord is my shepherd, not my bellhop. We should not confuse natural law and the activity of God (sometimes, alas! considered mechanical and called Law), but this has essentially nothing to do with the laws of nature, which are the habitual responses of experiences to God's giving. (Just reviewing a little, in case you forgot.)

Practical Purposes

Of course, you can visualize the way God operates or anything else you choose to visualize in any way that works for you, including images that don't match reality at all. The Simontons, a physician and a psychologist, got wonderful results with cancer patients given up as hopeless. They taught those patients to visualize their cancer in some fashion that illustrated the understanding that the cells of their immune system were much more powerful than the cancer cells, which are in fact weak and confused. One effective visualization was to imagine the cancerous cells as weeds in a grassy meadow and the immune system T-cells as hungry sheep mowing the lawn. Now those patients knew that there weren't any sheep in their bloodstream; it was just a myth, or metaphor. German philosopher Hans Vaihinger in his philosophy of "as if," called such metaphors "useful fictions." The great depth psychologist, Alfred Adler, was very taken with Vaihinger's philosophy. The idea is that you *act as if* certain things were literally true, even though they may not be, because it's useful to do so.

Now it's time to finish our treatment. We don't just visualize or argue for what we want and then jump up and walk away. *Phase Three* comes after we are thoroughly clear on what we want, and have visualized it until our doubts and fears dissolve and we feel the reality of our outcome. Former editor of *Cosmopolitan Magazine* Helen Gurley Brown once wrote, "You have to feel the mink around your shoulders." When Deb was working on her doctorate at Northern Illinois University, slaving away in the university library or on the computer, or taking comprehensive exams, she used to imagine the feel of the doctoral hood around her shoulders. Lo and behold, at commencement, the professors actually "hooded" the candidates on stage in a special ceremony. Of course, they got Deb's inside out, but it's the thought that counts.

Phase Three also emulates Jesus, who gave thanks in advance, showing his trust in the power of God. When you order an automobile to be built at the factory, you thank the salesperson in advance for something that doesn't yet exist except as an idea in mind, but you just *know* that that car is on its way to you. Or you thank the architect who draws the blueprints for a house that as yet exists only in people's imaginations. In this spirit of expectancy, you cultivate the attitude of gratitude that is one of the hallmarks of people who are prosperous and affluent enough to be happy and content. Process thinkers recognize that part of an experience looks toward the anticipated future.

Then you let go and let God. By aligning yourself with God, you have opened a channel through which abundance can flow to you and on to the world. In quiet confidence, assured of the outcome, you *give thanks* and *release* your request to the universe to be worked out under God's orchestration. Peter Marshall, former U.S. Senate chaplain and subject of the best-selling book, *A Man Called Peter*, used to tell a story about a little boy who takes his bicycle to the repair shop to be fixed, but instead of releasing it to the repairman in trust and going on about his business, the little boy pesters the repairman with endless questions and doubts, and generally gets in the way. All too often we do this to God. Instead, we must release our broken bicycle to the divine repairman with thanks and trust, and be on about our business so the repairman can work. That is Phase Three.

To recapitulate: Phase One of affirmative prayer is the preparation, the aligning of body, mind, and spirit with God. Phase Two is the statement of our desire and the anticipation of our desired outcome. Phase Three is the thankful release in happy expectation. That is how to use the Power of God in the

Practical Purposes

cocreation process that glorifies God and benefits us. Now let us look at the specific areas in which we most desire to cocreate.

Health

The practice of the presence of God for practical purposes needs to include regular attention to caring for the body through diet, exercise, and other wellness practices, as well as specific prayer treatment in times of illness. The physical body is an important part of one's spirituality, and it is a big mistake to think that one is more spiritual if one neglects the physical body. Many famous spiritual giants have died of horrible illnesses, due at least in part to the neglect of or contempt for the body. This is not maintaining proper balance. Stephen Covey's seventh Habit, *Sharpen the saw*, is about maintaining the balance among the physical, mental, spiritual, and social/emotional areas of life. Covey stresses the importance of daily attention to this balance. St. Paul said that the body is the temple of the Holy Spirit (1 Cor. 6:19). The body's own tendency toward balance is known as *homeostasis*. It works to maintain a reference setting of temperature, degree of acidity or alkalinity, and a host of other balances.

Healing begins literally before we know that we are ill or injured. The life in the body goes to work immediately when something disturbs the equilibrium of the body, the homeostasis. It has been said that the tendency of the subconscious is lifeward: healing tends to take place if we get ourselves out of the way. Getting out of the way consists of not thinking negative thoughts that depress our immune system, not eating foods that are inappropriate for our particular metabolism or have had the nutrients refined out of them, and not breathing foul air or tobacco smoke. No matter what your metabolic type is, eating many foods made with refined flour and sugar or with hydrogenated fats (which includes, sadly, most processed foods today) will sooner or later lead to illness, because the body isn't getting the necessary nutrients and is wasting nutrients in processing the junk. If you have no idea what your metabolic type is, dietician Ann Louise Gittleman has a book, *Your Body Knows Best*, that can help you determine and understand your type. Ayurvedic medicine also has information about various body types. For instance, the vegetarian diet that may be perfect for a slow metabolizer is unsuitable for a fast metabolizer, who needs more protein and fat for optimum wellness. Eating the wrong foods or the wrong ratio of protein, carbohydrate, and fat for your type can lead to obesity and lack of energy, and can make you more susceptible to illness.

We want more than the absence of illness; we want abundant wellness. This includes high energy levels, the absence of aches and pains, and a fit, supple body. To achieve wellness, we need to work in accordance with the natural physical laws by eating nutritious food, taking appropriate food supplements, and drinking plenty of water; by exercising our body in ways suited to that particular body; and by maintaining a balance of work and play, rest and activity. As in all other aspects of life, we must assume responsibility for our own wellness, not depending on physicians. Too many people wait until they're basket cases, then drag their bodies in to the doctor and expect him or her to fix them. But the doctor can't eat properly and exercise for you! Once again we hear Robert Schuller's words ringing in our ears, "If it's going to be, it's up to me."

Different body types differ in the type and quantity of exercise that is appropriate. Then, too, the exercise you choose should be an activity—or a variety of activities—that you enjoy. Some people enjoy sports and some don't. Some people feel pleasantly smoothed out by a yoga routine, others find it boring or too difficult. There's always walking, dancing, bicycling, swimming, or tai chi (a Chinese martial art in slow motion that can be practiced even in advanced old age. Divine Science minister Carmen Brockelhurst teaches a special form of Tai Chi that was developed just for reducing stress in the West and is easier to learn). Exercising with friends or family is a great way to combine goals for meeting physical and social needs. Research shows that if you exercise regularly, you'll live longer, stay healthier, and feel better.

Other important practices related to wellness are drinking a lot of pure water and breathing fresh air. We need six to eight glasses of water a day *in addition to* anything caffeinated, which dehydrates the body; or juices, which have nutritional value but do not substitute for plain water. Lack of water alone can cause serious illnesses. Deep breathing, pulling fresh air far down into the lungs and imagining it circulating through the body before exhaling, is vital to good health. The harm done by smoking is by now thoroughly demonstrated. If you are still a nicotine addict, seek help. There are numerous approaches available, from nicotine patches to hypnosis. Prayer treatment and visualization are important, because you need to see yourself as a non-smoker. What would it look like, sound like, or feel like, not to need nicotine? (Unfortunately, there is no positive name for a person who does not smoke. Deb's stepdaughter, Pamela Whitehouse, suggests *free airist*!)

Another important factor in wellness is family or other social ties. One famous study revealed that despite diets that were less than ideal, people that lived long and healthy lives were those with an abundance of social interaction: family, friends, church, community. So if you're a hermit, reach out and touch someone! There's always somebody worse off than you are, to whom you can be a blessing. One of the greatest gifts you can give someone is just to listen actively to that person.

Chapter Four

Frequently, the best advice on wellness comes from alternative sources, with the use of physicians best reserved for trauma and crises. Harvard-trained physician Andrew Weil, in his book, *Health and Healing*, covers the history of healing in our own culture and others. According to Weil, the ancient Chinese practice was to pay the physician only as long as one remained well and to stop paying him if one became sick! Some of the healthiest cultures have relied mainly on herbs and other natural remedies, turning to drugs or surgery only as a last resort. Although God is in the hands of the surgeon and in drugs as much as in herbs, reliance on prayer treatment and natural remedies seems to be the wisest approach for New Thoughters. Nobel prize-winning biochemist Roger Williams used to say, "Try nutrition first," and this is good advice.

We might add, "along with prayer." Physician Larry Dossey has collected studies indicating the efficacy of prayer. Dossey indicates that in some studies, prayer is shown to be so effective that if it were a drug being tested, the codes used in a double-blind study would be broken, and all patients would receive it. His book, *Prayer is Good Medicine*, documents the most recent efforts to demonstrate this. The most effective prayer, Dossey has learned, is "Thy will be done," leaving it to God to know what an individual's highest good is.

In case of illness, our daily visualization needs to include wellness, and our daily practice needs to add wise and well-researched healing methods that assist the lifeward tendency. One of the best healing methods is the form of prayer known as *treatment*: seeing God in place of the illness. Illness can be a great teacher, and we can ask God's guidance in learning its lesson so we don't have to repeat it. We can also use wellness affirmations as blueprints. The most famous is probably Emil Coué's "Every day in every way I am getting better and better."

Practical Purposes

New Thought began with the healing work of Phineas Parkhurst ("Park") Quimby well over a century ago. Quimby described his approach as "mind acting directly upon mind," his mind disputing with the mind of the patient the belief in illness. Over a period of years, he healed thousands of people, many of whom the physicians had given up on.

For Quimby, "the explanation is the cure." John Sarno, professor of clinical rehabilitation medicine at New York School of Medicine, uses a similar approach today to heal back pain with no medical intervention. In his book, *Healing Back Pain: The Mind-Body Connection*, he explains his method. His patients are required to attend one illustrated lecture on the back, in which they learn how a very real physical disorder can be induced by emotional phenomena, and that there is nothing "wrong" with their backs. He makes them give up all their treatment of symptoms and substitute relaxation instead. The overwhelming majority of his patients are successfully cured by this explanation alone.

Although Quimby abandoned the formal use of mesmerism fairly early in his career, he undoubtedly continued to use the skills he had acquired as a mesmerizer to aid people in going into an alpha state in which they could be most resourceful in their healing work on themselves. These techniques are now well understood and taught by numerous people from physician Herbert Benson to healer José Silva.

Most of the New Thought founders were involved in healing themselves. Charles and Myrtle Fillmore were both healed of serious and, in Myrtle's case, life-threatening infirmities. Ernest Holmes helped to heal his mother of a serious heart ailment early in his career. Malinda Cramer and Nona Brooks experienced healings. Some of these healings were nearly instantaneous; others took a long time to be completed. Most healings by prayer require a fairly long period of time and support of the healing process from diet, relaxation, and other means of building wellness.

In the last analysis, divinely guided life is doing the healing, not the physician, the herb or drug, or even the patient. We can say yes to God's perfect healing possibilities by giving our attention to wellness and by operating in accordance with the physical and mental laws of the universe. In this way, moment by moment, we reduce the difference between the pattern of the past and the wellness we desire.

When we are in pain or upset, often it is easier for someone else to visualize us as well and at peace than it is for us to do so ourselves. Here is where a healer or practitioner can be helpful. Further, some individuals apparently have special healing powers that are not fully understood. Such people frequently work by the laying on of hands. Unusual energy has been measured in the hands of some healers. Here, too, God is at work.

If you are experiencing a health challenge, the first step is to do whatever obvious thing you can to improve your health: get more rest, reduce stress, improve your diet, exercise if your physical condition permits. In case of acute or life-threatening illness, you may need to consult a physician, but you are the ultimate expert on your body and your life. It may be helpful to ask yourself what message this particular illness has for you, what it is here to teach you. As we have indicated before, blame is useless, as is seeing yourself as a victim. You can, however, notice if you are doing something obvious to contribute to your illness, and if you are, stop doing it! In 90 percent of illnesses, the cause is mental, but even if the cause is not immediately apparent, changing your mind to focus on wellness is helpful. If you are focusing on wellness, you will be making plans to eat properly, rest, relax, and exercise appropriately, and you will be picturing wellness. All this will be helpful, even if the immediate cause of the illness is not poor diet or lack of exercise.

It is important to think holistically: mind and body are parts of the same system, and what affects one affects the other. Reality Therapist Ed Ford likes to point out that in a hospital emergency room, there is a definite order of seriousness in which conditions are addressed first, breathing, next, heartbeat, and so on. In the psychological arena, one might begin the healing process with something equivalent in importance on the emergency room scale to capping a tooth. That one little change might be enough to begin an important shift in consciousness.

Some form of prayer treatment, either alone or with the help of a practitioner, is always a good idea. Many people have cured many ailments by using prayer treatment for a long enough time. However, there are times when it is quicker and hence more appropriate to take aspirin or the equivalent and keep going. Don't kid yourself, though. If the ailment recurs frequently, you would be foolish to ignore it.

In New Thought, there is a saying: There are no accidents. This is particularly true of health challenges. Contrary to appearances, we do not get zapped out of the blue by some bug. Bugs are present in our bodies all the time, held in check and balance by our immune system. If the immune system gets run down by stress, poor lifestyle, or negative thinking, the bugs get the upper hand. A stiff or sore neck can be a bodily reflection of a person or situation that we perceive to be a "pain in the neck." New Thought minister Louise Hay has a number of books dealing with the way that illness is an outpicturing of something that is going on in the mind. Don't carry this too far, though, and get into blaming the victim for having a rotten consciousness, especially if the victim is you! As Sigmund Freud, arguably the most famous perceiver of hidden meanings, observed, "Sometimes a cigar is just a cigar," and sometimes an illness is just an illness, and doesn't need psychoanalyzing. In that case, just concentrate on wellness. If there is a lesson you need to be learning from your illness, it will usually become apparent fairly quickly.

The great idea that healed Unity cofounder Myrtle Fillmore of what was believed to be hereditary tuberculosis was, "I am a child of God and I do not inherit sickness." What we may inherit is a higher than normal requirement for a particular nutrient, the lack of which may lead to a certain illness. Or we may inherit bad eating habits or other lifestyle habits. Habits we can do something about, though it isn't always easy.

Another contributing factor to illness is secondary gain: the benefits you derive out of being sick. Maybe you enjoy being waited on, get out of going to a job you hate, or avoid having to do housework you don't enjoy. Many a child has developed an illness to stay home from school with. It is very important to ask yourself what you gain from your illness. Adler used to ask his patients, "What would you do, or what would it be like, if you didn't have this illness?" and then listen carefully to the response, which might reveal what the patient was using the illness to avoid. If, on the other hand, the response was something like "It wouldn't hurt when I get up in the morning," secondary gain was probably not involved.

Some people enjoy poor health. They take a sour pleasure in complaining about their ailments, and keep their attention on those ailments most of the time. It brings them sympathy and attention from others, and gives them an excuse for not accomplishing anything worthwhile with their lives. These are all secondary gains. Such people may not know how to get love

Practical Purposes

from others by more positive means. If you fall into this category, remember first of all that you have God's unconditional love at all times, and that God wants you to be well and happy. Then try to find something loving to do for someone else to help you get your mind off your own health challenges. That alone can lead to miraculous healings. There is a story about a woman who was bedridden in Hawaii at the time of the attack on Pearl Harbor. Because she was staying in one place, she became a message center for keeping people in touch with one another through the confusion, and as she became more and more involved in the effort, she gained strength, forgot her illness, and was soon out of bed, completely well again.

Even if, for some reason, bodily healing (cure) is not possible, inner healing can still take place, so that a person is at peace with him or herself and with the illness. This type of healing is a mental and spiritual shift of great power. However, many people who could otherwise be cured believe that cure is impossible, so for them, it is.

It is extremely important to ask yourself, "Do I sincerely want to be healed?" If the answer is no, you have some work to do on your internal congruence before you can do much to seek bodily healing. Jesus said repeatedly, "Thy faith hath made thee whole" (Matt. 9:22, Mark 5:34, 10:52, Luke 8:48, 17:19), and on at least one occasion asked, "Wilt thou be made whole?" (John 5:6).

Above all, the main ingredient necessary for healing is love replacing thoughts of fear or hatred with thoughts of love for yourself, for your body, especially the part of it that is out of whack, and for everyone else in your life. Healing is closely linked to forgiveness, which means getting out of your consciousness any thought that you have been wronged by anyone. You don't have to condone wrong actions, just release the perpetrator from your thinking (even if it's you!) by wishing him or her well, and get on with your life. You can choose to operate in such a way that you are both less vulnerable and more tolerant of the foibles of others in the future, just as you can choose to take better care of your body. Jesus astonished bystanders by healing a paralytic with the words "Be of good cheer, your sins are forgiven you." Sin, missing the mark, can have a negative effect on the body, because all of our actions, physical and mental, have consequences. To the cripple whom he healed at the pool of Bethesda, Jesus said, "See, you have been made well. Sin no more, lest a worse thing befall you." (John 5:14)

Wealth

God is the source of all wealth, for God "gives you power to get wealth" (Deut. 8:18). We are filled to overflowing with the abundance of God, which then goes from us out into the world. As Unity's Jim Rosemergy puts it, the real prosperity demonstration is giving, not getting "God is the source. Awareness of it is your supply." This abundance concept is the antidote to belief in lack or a need to compete for scarce resources. Jesus did not say rob the rich to feed the poor. He said that the poor have the Gospel (good news) preached to them (Matt. 11:5, Luke 7:22). The good news is that they, too, can develop a prosperity consciousness.

Wealth, as well as all else, involves understanding that as Jesus said, "it is the Father's good pleasure to give you the kingdom" (Luke 12:32), that there is plenty for all, and that all deserve to prosper. At the same time, we can be good stewards of the environment, knowing that God gives the increase if we do our part. Our practice for wealth includes learning about money and how it works, managing properly whatever money we have at present, regarding wealth and the wealthy in a

Practical Purposes

positive way, expecting to prosper, and visualizing ourselves and others as prospering. God wants us to do what we love and to prosper by doing it, so with the help of God's wisdom, we can find a need and fill it (or better still, create a need and fill it) as a means of gaining wealth.

Prosperity has been defined in New Thought as peace of mind, health of body, harmonious relationships, and abundant successful living. Money alone cannot make you prosperous if other areas of your life are out of balance. Talk show host Oprah Winfrey has interviewed winners of big lottery payoffs who were thoroughly miserable despite all their money. The amount of money needed for happiness—and everyone needs some money—varies from person to person, depending on goals and interests. Some projects require a lot of money. With a lot of money comes the responsibility for looking after it, which some people enjoy and some don't. If you have that mansion and yacht you always dreamed of, you either have to oversee a large payroll of servants, hire someone to oversee a large payroll of servants and then oversee the overseer yourself, or run yourself ragged trying to keep up with it all by yourself. Are you willing to put up with the hassle, or would your purposes be served by temporarily renting the yacht or the mansion, perhaps for a vacation? So the first step in prosperity as in everything else is to get very clear in your own mind just what you really want. Then you can determine how much money you need to make it work out. It may be less than you think!

The next step in attaining prosperity is to heal your poverty consciousness. Healing a poverty consciousness is much the same as healing a bodily ailment: you must change your mind and keep the change (which happens to be the title of a book on neuro-linguistic programming, NLP for short). Many, if not most of us, are programmed for poverty in childhood. We "inherit" ideas of lack and limitation from our parents, who think they are just being realistic about there not being enough to go around. Did you grow up on sayings such as "Money doesn't grow on trees," "I'm not made of money," and other limiting notions? *Step one* in healing a poverty consciousness is to become aware of and get rid of such ideas. Other harmful ideas involve the belief that you do not deserve to prosper, or that rich people are evil or selfish (in that case, you'd hate yourself if you became rich!) Many people still believe that God doesn't want them to be rich. God is not glorified by poverty, but by your becoming the best you can be. In a culture that uses money, that takes money.

Money is neither good nor evil. It has value because we say it does. It is a convenient substitute for barter, and it is a secondary gain, meaning that we seek it for the sake of what we can buy with it, not for itself. Even gold or silver is not much use when you are hungry, unless you can exchange it for food. Money is governed by rules, just as everything else is; for example, "Dig the well before you are thirsty" translated to money means to set aside the money you are going to need in the future now, before you need it. In other words, plan ahead.

The best advice for managing money is to start by managing well whatever money you do have, using it in correct proportions to cover the various areas of your life, such as food, shelter, and transportation. Also, picture yourself with the lifestyle you desire, paid for in full. The more you visualize, the more ordinary your good fortune will feel when it arrives. If you feel that you are playing over your head, or that you don't deserve to prosper, you will not be able to keep money even if you manage to acquire some.

As with everything else, money grows when you give your attention to it. Learn about banking and investments, and by all means learn how the income tax system works, so that you can legally minimize what you fork over to Uncle Sam. It's not patriotic to overpay; it's stupid!

The real bottom line is that God gives the increase. You are not depriving anyone else of prosperity by prospering yourself; in fact, you are helping others by enriching the background from which their next occasions of experience arise. Putting it another way, the ship that comes home to your neighbor comes home to you, and there goes the neighborhood—straight up! Never create a poverty consciousness by envying anyone's good fortune: if others can succeed, so can you. Sincerely congratulate others on their good fortune, and picture the day when they are similarly congratulating you.

Some years ago, business consultant Marsha Sinetar wrote a book with the title, *Do What You Love: The Money Will Follow*. It's true. Your greatest loves come from God, and God wants you to make the most of them. It's no glory to God to have you slaving in a job that makes you miserable. It's no glory to God to have you scrimping and saving just to survive. Jesus said, "I am come that they might have life, and that they might have it more abundantly" (John 10:10). He didn't say anything about scraping by, living meagerly or stingily. The best way to prosper is to find out what you love to do, what you would happily do all day even if you didn't get paid for it, and then find a way to do that, even if at first you can only do it occasionally or part time. Then look for opportunities to prosper doing that. A few people whose love doesn't pay well have had to earn a living doing something else in order to support doing what they love, but most of us can eventually work things so that we spend the majority of our time doing what we do best and love best.

Another important thing to understand about money is that increase is directly tied to the number of transactions, so you have to get out and make things happen where people are. And you have to identify perceived needs, because people aren't going to pay you for satisfying a need that they don't know they have.

New Thought psychologist Robert Anthony points out that the easiest way to succeed is to go from being to doing to having. The world has it backward: it thinks that in order to be a ballerina, you have to have a tutu and lessons, and then if you do what ballerinas do (practice), you will eventually get to be a ballerina. This may work, but it's doing it the hard way. Anthony illustrates this point with the story of a little girl who wants to be a singer. In her little ragged dress and bare feet, she sings you a song and she's being a singer, doing what singers do, which is sing. Eventually, a talent scout hears her and gets her a vocal coach, costumes, and bookings, so she then has what singers have, including fame, flowers, curtain calls, and money.

None of this violates the essential process principle that becoming or activity is basic, that there is no being except as abstracted or derived from becoming. Being quiet is just one form of activity, however subtle it may be.

As in everything else, the key to money and overall prosperity is in what you give your attention to. If you are thinking about your bills, how much you hate your job, the poverty you grew up in, or the poverty you are currently surrounded with, then you are perpetuating these conditions with your thoughts. In process terms, you are building up a negative past that makes it more difficult for you to accept God's offer of prosperity. Prosperity experts recommend finding ways to surround yourself with luxury, even if it's by hanging out in the lobby of a fine hotel or bank, or test driving an expensive car, just to give yourself the feel of what it would be like to be rich. It is also important to praise and give thanks for whatever you do have, even if it's a house with a leaky roof or a car with the doors rusted out. Find something good to say or think about it, and take as good care of it as if it were a BMW so that you'll know how to treat one when you get it.

Here again we see that all areas of our lives are interconnected, and that details do matter. Your brain hears what your mouth says. What you bless, you prosper, and the balky old car is a lot more likely to keep running if you praise it. The same is true of your body, your spouse, and your rhododendron. A wonderful sign that mysteriously appears over photocopy machines warns of the importance of speaking kindly to the machine and working patiently, expecting good results, or it is likely to get sulky and jam on you, in which case it is no use going to another machine, because they all belong to the same union!

Author Phil Laut outlines four laws of wealth in his book, *Money Is My Friend*:

1. THE EARNING LAW: All human wealth is created by the human mind. The application of *the earning law* involves the pleasurable creation of sufficient income.
2. THE SPENDING LAW: The value of money is determined by the buyer and seller in every transaction. Application of *the spending law* involves enjoyment of the things that you spend money for.
3. THE SAVING LAW: The accumulation of a surplus from your income. Application of *the saving law* results in an attitude of abundance, which you can expect to see reflected in your future income.
4. THE INVESTING LAW: Spending your capital in your name for the purpose of increasing your income. Application of *the investing law* is a combination of all three laws of wealth, as the factors of earning, spending, and saving all come into play.

As in all visualization, specificity is important. You want a certain sum of money for a particular purpose. Visualize that sum and that purpose, and note the deadline by which you need the money. Perhaps you might picture a wall calendar showing the date as you deposit a check for the amount of money you need to pay certain bills, or you imagine yourself purchasing the item you have longed for, paying for it in full, so you do not incur debt. With the possible exception of house mortgages and car payments, debt tends to give you a sense of burden, and leads to poverty consciousness. If you are currently in debt, Thing One is to make a careful plan to pay it off as quickly as possible while maintaining a reasonable quality of life. In most cases, the interest on the debt is higher than the interest on an investment would be, so your best investment is in paying off the debt. After you are debt free, various financial experts can guide you to next steps, usually owning a home, some modest insurance, and then an investment program. The goal is to get to where your investment income surpasses your earned income and you can retire to do what you love, financially independent. In all this, of course, you can ask for God's guidance at each choice point.

Some people question whether it is spiritual to prosper. Catherine Ponder is emphatic on this point: she says it is "shockingly *right* rather than shockingly wrong for you to prosper." Charles Fillmore flatly stated that poverty is a sin, meaning that you are falling far short of the mark that you should achieve as the child of a rich heavenly Father. We have heard New Thought minister Johnnie Colemon say, "God *wants* you to have that Cadillac. *He* certainly doesn't need it!" If you are leading a principle-centered, character-based life, as Stephen Covey recommends, your transactions will be win-win, and so everything you do will be assisting others to prosper as well as yourself.

Practical Purposes

In 1915 a poor farmer named Wallace D. Wattles, who had risen to become a successful educator and teacher of New Thought principles, published a book, *The Science of Getting Rich*. In it, he states:

> Man's right to life means his right to have the free and unrestricted use of all the things which may be necessary to his fullest mental, spiritual, and physical unfoldment; or, in other words, his right to be rich. In this book, I shall not speak of riches in a figurative way; to be really rich does not mean to be satisfied or contented with a little. No man ought to be satisfied with a little if he is capable of using and enjoying more. The purpose of Nature is the advancement and unfoldment of life; and every man should have all that can contribute to the power, elegance, beauty, and richness of life; to be content with less is sinful. . . . It is perfectly right that you should desire to be rich; if you are a normal man or woman you cannot help doing so. It is perfectly right that you should give your best attention to the Science of Getting Rich, for it is the noblest and most necessary of all studies. If you neglect this study, you are derelict in your duty to yourself, to God, and to humanity; for you can render God and humanity no greater service than to make the most of yourself.

To attain wealth, Wattles explains, you must think and act in a certain way. Thinking in a certain way is clearly visualizing exactly what you want. Acting in a certain way means doing each day all that you can do toward your goals without worrying about the past or the future, getting what you want by giving the other person what is his or hers. Wattles emphasizes, "Do not wait for a change of environment before you act, get a change of environment by action." He explains that we must pass from the competitive to the creative mind, holding a clear mental picture of the things we want, with the fixed purpose to get what we want, and the unwavering faith that we do get what we want.

David Cates, in his book, *Unconditional Money*, tells how he went from flat broke to financially independent by working as a butler to the rich and famous, asking them to tell him their wealth secrets. He also had numerous mystical experiences along the way. He describes one such experience:

> I saw that everything is, and always was, and always will be, absolute perfection. Nothing is finished, yet nothing's left undone. I could appreciate the beauty of each thread, each life, the love that's shining in each dream we've given to the whole. I came to see that God was dreaming in us, and through us. All God does is dream creation into being. Creation is the key. Until we consciously join in that process, God will only be a distant presence, and we mere victims at the hand of fate. . . . Once I move into the miracle of cocreation, we're all one. Everything is possible. We're doing this together.

This reference to becoming one in cocreation probably was written without knowledge of the structure of experience as presented in process thought, but it expresses rather well the fusion of divine purpose with the influence of the past as a result of one's free choice.

Self-made millionaire Mark Fisher tells of his own wealth lessons in a fictionalized account, *The Instant Millionaire*. The millionaire gardener who mentors him teaches him to be specific about the amount of money he wants, to seize opportunities, and to take risks. "The young man" who is the hero of the tale also must learn to have faith to overcome his recurring doubts and to

Practical Purposes

focus on a goal. He also learns the value of self-image, when the millionaire tells him,

> The greatest obstacle to success is a mental obstacle. Expand your mental limits and you will expand the limits of your life. Explode your limitations and you will explode the limitations of your life. The conditions in your life will change as if by magic. I swear by experience this is true. . . . The world is but a reflection of your inner self. The conditions in your life are but a mirror image of your inner life.

Referring to one of his prize roses, the millionaire continues,

> Concentrate on the heart of the rose and there you will find truth and the intuition you will need to guide you through life. You will also find the dual secret of true wealth: love for whatever you do, and love for others.

The young man also learns to live each day as if it were his last, living it to the fullest by doing what he wants to do. He learns the old saying, "Character equals destiny." "Strengthen your mind, and circumstances will yield to your desires," the millionaire tells him. "You will gain control over your own life." And finally, "Be still, and know that I am God."

These lessons do us no good if we merely agree with them intellectually. We must put the learnings to work, must experience them for ourselves. Otherwise, the old poverty thoughts keep us paralyzed in our poverty consciousness. We have to build the mental equivalent of prosperity, feel the mink around our shoulders, smell the new car smell, picture ourselves easily affording the house or the boat or the swing set for the kids. We have to see and feel ourselves as deserving of beauty and luxury, and to understand that we wish the same for everyone else, that we are not depriving anyone by getting what we want as long as we practice win-win or no deal in all our transactions.

The one thing we cannot have is someone else's wealth, because we have to visualize our own. Envy, which is sorrow at someone else's good fortune, or coveting someone else's good, will keep our own good away from us, because in both cases our consciousness is filled with thoughts of what we lack. "Them that has, gets," because they have it in consciousness. Jesus taught this principle in the parable of the talents, and it has puzzled many people who thought it sounded unfair. The servant who hid his talent in the ground instead of putting it to work to earn more money got chewed out by his lord (Matt. 25:26-30).

The principles of wealth will serve us just as well as any of the other principles, if we live by them.

Happiness

Doing what we love, or even visualizing and planning to be able to do what we love at some future date, helps ensure happiness. Happiness is a state of enhanced satisfaction. If we are using our talents to fill others' needs by doing what we love and doing it well, we will be well on our way to a satisfying life. We can seek to understand and to have win-win relationships with those we love. And we can become very clear about what we want, visualize it, and work with interest to attain it. Success can be defined as achieving what you set out to do.

We had a lot to say about the research on happiness in our first book. To summarize, people are happiest when they are able to lose themselves in the flow of some worthwhile activity, not when they are watching television or otherwise vegging out.

Practical Purposes

Happiness is not a mood, but a function associated with the left-hemisphere of the brain. We become happy by choosing to be happy, to note what we are satisfied with at present, and enhancing our satisfaction by dwelling on the details of it.

For example, we recently got a new car after many years of driving a small, cramped, no-frills rustmobile. Our pleasure in the new car is enhanced by our noticing the beautiful, polished, blemish-free finish, the quiet purr of the powerful engine, the comfort of the seats, the little improvements in the design of the seat belts and interior lights, and of course, the marvelous new-car smell! Dwelling on the details of our satisfaction with our new car creates a state of happiness every time we ride in it. Just driving to the grocery store with Bach playing on the FM stereo is like taking a vacation! Alan's favorite feature is the trip odometer: he clocks the distance to the grocery store. Well, we all find our happiness in different ways.

Abraham Lincoln observed, "People are about as happy as they make up their minds to be," and it's true. Surprisingly, people who have undergone some terrible physical affliction that leaves them paralyzed or without a limb are usually happy, because they have come to terms with their condition. Happiness also involves feeling that one is of service to others, and one can find ways of serving others even when one is paralyzed and bedridden. Here is where good character comes into play in terms of persisting until difficulties are overcome.

Happiness is a choice, as many people have pointed out. You can choose to look for the benefits in a situation, or at least the humor. Such an attitude empowers you to be more creative and resourceful, and you are more likely to come out of the situation with a solution to your problems. Happiness is closely allied with optimism and with positive expectancy. You will be happy if you are completely engrossed in the present moment, and that is something you can choose to be. People often push their happiness into the future by saying, "I will be happy when I get married," or get a certain house or car or promotion. But why postpone happiness? Choose to be happy now as well as in the future.

Barry Neil Kaufman, in his book, *Happiness is a Choice*, lists three reasons why people are afraid to be happy. *First*, they fear that if they were happy all the time, they would become idiotic or at least dull of brain. Yet, as Kaufman points out, "Dispensing with unhappiness is the single most significant activity we can undertake in any effort to sharpen our minds and enhance our ability to think."

The *second* reason that people are afraid to be happy is that they believe they would lack initiative, energy, and conviction, that they would lose their clear vision. "In contrast," says Kaufman, "happiness bubbles forth from an optimistic, hopeful vision of the universe. Unencumbered by the anchor of misery, happier people move decisively and energetically. . . Happiness is power! Happiness is self-empowerment."

The *third* reason that people are afraid to be happy is that they fear that they would be insensitive, because they have learned to associate happiness with superficiality and insensitivity. If we are unhappy, we must care deeply. But as Kaufman notes, if we take on the sadness of another, "what we have then is two sad people," or two angry people, if we take on another's anger at some injustice. "Happiness," Kaufman indicates, "might, in fact, be the most sensitive and useful tool with which to assist someone we love through a difficult circumstance."

Kaufman repeats the basic truth that all of us always do what we take to be our best, in accordance with our beliefs. If you change the beliefs, the behaviors and feelings resulting from those beliefs will change, too. Kaufman has interviewed child molesters, pathological liars, and others whose behavior the world views as extremely objectionable. In every case, he found that the person had been well-intentioned. By respecting the underlying intention, he has been able to get even such people to change their behavior, though they of course still had to face the consequences of it. "We are the architects of our own attitudes and experiences. We design the world by the way we choose to see it!" he states.

Kaufman has an earlier book with the title *To Love is to Be Happy With*. He picks up that theme in *Happiness is a Choice*:

> When we are happy with ourselves, we are accepting of ourselves (not judging ourselves). When we are happy with others, we are accepting of them (not judging others). Happiness brings us closer together rather than pushing us apart. But above all, happiness makes love tangible. To love someone fully and completely is to be happy with that person, to accept him without judgments and celebrate our own existence. . . . We can become the gift-givers to others and ourselves, and the gift we can offer is our happiness and the peace, love and acceptance that flow from it.

How do we choose happiness? By making it a priority, says Kaufman. Certainly this "to love is to be happy with" approach is what Jesus taught "This is my commandment, that you love one another as I have loved you" (John 15:12). He also admonished, "Judge not, that ye be not judged" (Matt. 7:1)

Chapter Four

Relationships

If to love is to be happy with, and love is wishing someone well, then we have our guidelines for relationships. Three of Covey's Seven Habits deal with relationships, and together they constitute what Covey calls our Public Victory. Habit Four says to practice win-win or no deal, and the way we achieve this is with Habit Five, seeking first to understand before seeking to be understood. Habit Six, synergy, teaches us to value the differences between ourselves and others and to use those differences to attain something greater than either side could have come up with on its own. In our careers or our personal lives, these relationship guidelines work.

Before we can get very far with the Public Victory habits, we must have at least begun work on the Private Victory, Habits One, Two, and Three. These habits have us taking responsibility for our lives and committing to being principle-centered in our dealings. We will also have given thought to the nature of the universe, and, convinced of its abundance, are willing to practice win-win because we are sure that in an abundant, God-inspired universe, nobody has to lose.

Seeking first to understand will help us greatly in our relationships because we will learn that men are from Mars, and women are from Venus, as author John Gray tells us in his best-selling book with that title. To deal with these strange beings from another planet, we need to understand the customs of that planet and act accordingly. They are then more likely to be willing to understand us. Or if your boss has a Myers-Briggs type or an Enneagram number (personality indicators) at odds with yours, understanding those differences helps you to be more tolerant and meet the boss's needs. The boss in turn may look favorably on your performance when it is time for a raise.

Practical Purposes

There is a story about two sisters who were squabbling over the last orange in the house. Their quarrel ended when they learned that one needed the rind for a cake and the other wanted the juice. Had King Solomon himself come in with a decree that the orange be divided in half, nobody would have been happy. Another version of Habit Five is "Diagnose before you prescribe." An optometrist, as Covey points out, would look worse than foolish if he handed you his own glasses without measuring your eyes, saying, "Here, try these. They work well for me."

Sales trainer Tony Alessandra has a Platinum Rule, which, he says, is an improvement on the Golden Rule. The Platinum Rule says to do unto others as they would like to be done unto, which may not be what you would like done unto you at all. This is part of the secret of successful relationships, and it also operates through Habit Five. Much of the time, it's no skin off your nose to give the other person what he or she wants, and it pays big dividends.

Divine Guidance

All of us at times yearn for illumination, for guidance, for enlightenment. "Thy word is a lamp unto my feet," says Psalm 119:105, speaking of God. In symbolic interpretation of the Bible, feet symbolize understanding.

God speaks to us directly and indirectly all the time, for God is present in each occasion of experience. Intuitives, also called psychics, tell us that everyone is intuitive, but the trick is to interpret what one intuits, because intuitive messages usually come in pictures or symbols that we discount, ignore, or just plain don't understand. We assume that God speaks only in a clap of thunder, or in typical human ways of communicating. But "My ways are not your ways," says God in Isaiah 55:8.

Chapter Four

Sometimes we wish that God would just write a message in the sky saying Do this, but God isn't going to do that because it abrogates our free will. God only suggests, lures, leads, never forces. Sounds pretty exasperating to us, but God has infinite patience and love. God also has all the natural laws on God's side, helping to pull us into line. In the 23rd Psalm, the "rod and staff" that "comfort" are symbols of discipline. If we do not discipline ourselves, the laws of the universe will discipline us. Catherine Ponder explains,

> The shepherd's rod was a branch cut from a bush or tree, used for chastising the sheep when they tried to stray. The rod kept them in line. The shepherd carried a staff as a symbol of rank, power, authority, strength. . . . When you are making progress on any level of life, change comes. As it does, you must discipline yourself in order to receive the good, the blessing, from that change.

Such discipline is a comfort because it provides boundaries for us. It teaches us the way to walk in, guides "our feet into the way of peace" (Luke 1:79).

If we have a parent-child or senior-junior partner relationship with God, our lines of communication are open. We know that God loves us, cares about us, and wants the highest good for us, that God has given us our desires and will help us attain them. When we relax body and mind, we are better able to heed the still, small voice of God's guidance, whether we interpret it as God, an angel, a spirit guide, or Jiminy Cricket. Neale Donald Walsh, in his book, *Conversations With God*, records the following dialogue between God and himself, which came to him in automatic writing (We need to have a word with Walsh about not calling God *It*, but God is so loving and understanding that it doesn't seem to bother God).

Practical Purposes

If there really is a God, and You are It, why do You not reveal Yourself in a way we can all understand?

I have done so, over and over. I am doing so again right now.

No. I mean by a method of revelation that is incontrovertible; that cannot be denied.

Such as?

Such as appearing right now before my eyes.

I am doing so right now.

Where?

Everywhere you look. . . . So go ahead now. Ask Me anything. *Anything.* I will contrive to bring you the answer. The whole universe will I use to do this. So be on the lookout. This book is far from My only tool. You may ask a question, then *put this book down*. But watch. Listen. The words to the next song you hear. The information in the next article you read. The story line of the next movie you watch. The chance utterance of the next person you meet. Or the whisper of the next river, the next ocean, the next breeze that caresses your ear—all these devices are Mine; all these avenues are open to Me. I will speak to you if you will listen. I will come to you if you will invite Me. I will show you then that I have *always* been there. *All ways.*

The truth—and God knows it—is that even if God were to appear in some gee-whiz fashion, there would always be some people who were unconvinced or didn't recognize God or God's communication. Jesus built this into his parable of irresponsible rich man Dives and beggar Lazarus, who both died. Dives, in torment in Hades (presumably a cut-off-from-God state of consciousness), lifting his eyes and seeing Lazarus in Abraham's bosom, asks Abraham to at least send Lazarus to warn his five brothers to clean up their acts so they don't end up as he has. Abraham replies that if they don't believe Moses and the prophets, they aren't going to be persuaded even by someone rising from the dead. (Luke 17:19-31)

To communicate with God, just be still.

5. The Black Hole

In order to have positive thinking, there has to be the possibility of negative thinking, or how would you know that it was negative? If everything were light, with no shadows, it would be difficult or even impossible to see. So, in a book about the practice of the presence of God for practical purposes, there needs to be a chapter on negative thinking viewed through a New Thought filter, a sort of first-aid kit of ideas for what to do when things go wrong. In short, a visit to the metaphorical Black Hole, and instructions for getting out of it again.

Evil

Numerous theological tomes have been written on the problem of evil. This is sometimes known as theodicy (we don't have any idea what happened to theiliad). The *first* thing to note about evil is that it is only a problem if a) there is a God, and b) that God is good, because then how do you explain all this evil? If there is no God, or God is nasty or capricious, evil is what you would expect, and you would expect evil to be at least as plentiful as good. The *second* thing to note about evil is that the term is used to apply to things that human beings (and any other persons there may be) do to screw things up.

We are concerned here with what is called *moral evil*, resulting from deliberate acts of rational beings. Philosophers do not refer to hurricanes, earthquakes, tidal waves, or volcanic eruptions as morally evil, even though their consequences may be harmful. They use the term *natural evils*. Natural evils are part of a neutral environment in which it raineth both on the just and on the unjust whenever there is a low pressure system in the vicinity.

Evil resulting from the limitations of existence is what philosophers call *metaphysical evil*. (But you don't really care, do you?)

If there is no God, it is even tougher to explain the good and the order that are to be found in the world than it is to explain the evil to be found in the world with a good God, so we'll stay with the latter.

The *third* thing to note about evil is that, since it involves persons, it is relative. That means that there is no absolute force for evil, no evil personified, no Devil. Evil is the absence of good just as darkness is the absence of light or coldness is the absence of heat. When you walk into a dark room and turn on the light, you don't have to chase the darkness away; it simply vanishes in the light. So evil is relative to good just as darkness is relative to light, or cold to heat.

From a process point of view, evil has to do with might-have-beens. They are the result of choosing less of the good that God offers than one could have selected. To the extent that an experience actualizes any God-given possibilities, it is good. Evil is what could have been better.

Problems and difficulties are not evil per se. If we had no problems, we would be not only bored, but weak. If you try to help a baby chick peck its way out of the shell by making a hole in the shell, the baby chick will never develop its muscles and nerves properly through struggling. The same is true of a butterfly coming out of its cocoon: if you help it, you will damage it permanently and it will die prematurely. There is a folk tale about a village that made a bargain with God to get whatever growing conditions it asked for in order to have excellent crops. So the villagers prayed for sun and rain and mild weather. But because they failed to pray for the cold north wind to toughen the seedlings, the crops turned out poorly. The real power in life, the real satisfaction, comes in seeing oneself as a superb problem solver, not as some passive, dependent wimp who has no problems.

The Black Hole

Norman Vincent Peale used to point out that there were some people with no problems at all right down the road—in the cemetery. (Of course, we don't believe that there are any people in cemeteries, only the last of a long series of bodies that those people occupied during their earthly life. Physiologists tell us that our bodies get a complete change of cells every eleven months, or three years, or however long they say, this week, that it takes.) Then, we could get into a discussion about problems that people may or may not encounter in the afterlife, but we'll save that for another book. Meanwhile, if you have a burning desire to hear the arguments for and against life after death, you can read Alan's book, *More Than Mortal?*, available from the author. But we digress. (It's more fun that way.)

Then what *is* evil? In summary, practically put, most evil is the undesirable result of bad choices. If someone is not free to choose, we would not call him or her evil, even though the results of that person's actions might be. Evil results from our having free will, freedom to choose, and making choices that are not for our own highest good or someone else's highest good. Our choices can interfere with ourselves or others. Some people in New Thought like to define evil as immature or distorted good, and this captures the idea. Unity minister Greg Barrette tells us in his audio tape, *The Tao of Unity*, "Evil does exist as an effect, but not as a cause. It does not exist intrinsically as a permanent reality identified in and of itself, only as the relative absence of good."

Process thought adds perspective to this view of evil. In their book, *Process Theology: An Introductory Exposition*, John Cobb and David Griffin point out that in traditional Christianity, God was understood as the Cosmic Moralist, in other words, the Giant Cop in the Sky. Such a God was not interested in our enjoyment, which God at best only tolerated and at worst opposed. Moral goodness has been understood as suppressing

Chapter Five

much enjoyment. The notion of God as Cosmic Moralist is related to the idea of God as Controlling Power. If God controls all events and wills the maximum enjoyment for his creatures, then the problem of evil would disprove the existence of God, because all the suffering and inequalities in the world would suggest that God was "either malevolent or incompetent, if not both," say Cobb and Griffin. (Alan once put this in terms of God's being a weakie or a meanie.) So to save this old notion of God's being competently in control, one had to say that it's not a high priority for creatures to enjoy themselves, and perhaps God intends suffering to promote desired moral and religious attitudes.

In contrast to this old view, Cobb and Griffin state that

> Process theology sees God's fundamental aim to be the promotion of the creatures' own enjoyment. God's creative influence upon them is loving, because it aims at promoting that which the creatures experience as intrinsically good. Since God is not in complete control, the divine love is not contradicted by the great amount of intrinsic evil, or "disenjoyment," in the world. The creatures in part create both themselves and their successors.

Some traditional theism held that evil is only apparent, really a means to good, and therefore not genuinely evil. God as Controlling Power was *responsible* for evil but not *indictable* for it, since "all things work together for good." Process theology also sees God as responsible for evil but not indictable for it, but process theology doesn't deny that there is genuine evil: "there are events that would have been better otherwise, all things considered." Still, God is not indictable for this evil because 1) God's power is persuasive rather than controlling, and 2) the two forms of nonmoral evil are discord (physical or mental suffering) and *unnecessary* triviality. God's aim is to overcome unnecessary triviality while avoiding as much discord as possible; in other words, to aim for the perfection of experience. A third reason that God is not indictable for evil is that

> God's stimulation of a more and more complex world, which has the capacity for more and more intrinsic value, means the development of creatures with more and more freedom to reject the divine aims. Increased freedom in relation to the world necessarily means increased freedom in relation to God. . . . Hence . . . we can make ourselves miserable. . . . Also, we can form ourselves in such a way as to make ourselves objectively destructive elements in the environment of others. We can even do this deliberately—which is the essence of moral evil. Hence, increasing the freedom of the creatures was a risky business on God's part. But it was a necessary risk, if there was to be the chance for greatness.

Process thought teaches that because God suffers right along with us, God has even more motive than we do to prevent or ease suffering in the world. And God, like any loving parent, does not want God's children to suffer. So why doesn't God intervene? God can't intervene, because although God can lead and lure us, God cannot and would not violate our free will. God mitigates, but God cannot prevent evil. If God could prevent evil, we would be merely puppets. It's a much greater triumph for us to overcome evil than to be incapable of it, if that could be, which it can't, since freedom is essential in order for us to be.

We don't overcome evil by giving attention to it; that just makes it grow. We overcome evil by giving our attention to what we want, to the good. This is true of natural disasters as well. Even if an earthquake has wiped out a town, dwelling on the horrors will not help rebuild or relocate. What is needed is fresh dreams and new plans, and these God will provide. God also gives the increase: frequently, the new town is better than the old one ever could have been. It pays not to be too quick to judge an event as evil. It also pays not to build your town on a flood plain, a major fault line, or the slopes of a volcano.

There's a story from the Talmud about a rabbi and a rooster. The rabbi was walking along a road that ran along the edge of a forest. He was carrying a torch in one hand and had a rooster he was taking to market under his arm. Suddenly, the rooster jumped free and ran away. Did the rabbi curse his bad fortune or cry, "Why me, God?" No, he just observed to himself, "This will be for the good." Then, a while later, a gust of wind blew out his torch. Again the rabbi had faith and said to himself, "This will be for the good." With no torch to light his path, at dusk the rabbi left the road and went into the woods to sleep. He had no sooner settled himself quietly than a band of robbers came down the road and passed by without noticing him. Then it dawned on him that had he still had the torch and lit a campfire, the robbers would have spotted it, and he would have been beaten or killed. Had he still had the rooster, its noise would have attracted the robbers. Truly, the seemingly evil events had been for good.

Certainly, we need to be aware of what Deb as a psychologist calls current reality and Alan as a philosopher calls current actuality (translation: what's happening right now), to assess the situation and determine exactly where we are. If evil has been done to us, we need to look to see what we have left, not what we have lost.

The Black Hole

Did Brother Lawrence Have Bad Hair Days?

History tells us that Brother Lawrence emerged from the shadows into the sunlight after many years of persevering in his practice. Brother Lawrence may not have had bad hair days, but he undoubtedly dropped the dishes and maybe burned the biscuits on a few occasions. What did he do at such times? The same as he did the rest of the time: he practiced the presence of God by turning his attention to God and asking for God's help and guidance in his difficulty.

One thing about practice that it's important to understand is that it is a phase of an overall learning process that goes from not knowing and not knowing that we don't know (unconscious incompetence), to knowing that we don't know (conscious incompetence), to knowing in a shaky, self-conscious way (conscious competence), to operating on automatic pilot (unconscious competence). In the early stages of learning anything, we go through a confused, chaotic state, where anything we do right seems to be accidental, and we wonder if we'll ever get to mastery, ever learn to ride a two-wheeler or do differential calculus. If we stick with it, keep practicing until we get it right, then keep practicing it for its own sake (overlearning), we get to that wonderful state of unconscious competence that carries us along in the flow of events.

Still, we wrestle with our fears. Even if there is no power of darkness waiting to pounce on us, what about sin and evil, earthquakes and tidal waves, not to mention our own ignorance? To have free will, we must also have a neutral environment, a level playing field to exercise it in. If we can make it rain on you but not on us, that doesn't do much for your free will. So we have a universe that operates lawfully, and the laws affect everyone. That lawful universe happens to have hurricanes and volcanic eruptions, not to mention droughts, viruses, and plagues of locusts. God plays by the rules and cannot break them; however, God knows the laws and how they work better than anyone else, because God is directly or indirectly the source of the laws, just as God is the source of everything else. With God's guidance, you probably won't be there when the earthquake hits, or its effects will be mitigated in some way. When our consciousness is as it should be, aligned with God, we attract desirable conditions and avoid undesirable ones. Again, this is the power of the mind to affect everything in the universe, at least to some extent.

Then too, many people believe that this life is just one of many lives in which we realize our full potential and learn all the lessons we need to learn. This is the idea of reincarnation, but even without believing in reincarnation, many people still believe that the soul before birth chooses in at least a general way the experiences that it wants to have in this life in order to learn the lessons it needs to learn. In other words, we choose our parents and to some extent, our circumstances. Therefore, it is possible that we chose to experience, or at any rate, not to avoid, some evil or misfortune for the sake of the lessons it teaches. Or perhaps we have some unfinished business from a previous life (if such there be), some sin to atone for, some lesson to learn, or someone else that we may somehow assist or teach by our suffering in the present. This is where our faith in God comes in: to have faith that we are going to live forever somewhere, as Emmet Fox puts it, and that wherever we are, God is guiding and loving us. Despite appearances at any given moment, things are working out as they should, according to the divine plan, which is very flexible.

Sin, Original and Unoriginal, Which It Mostly Is

This brings us to the subject of sin, that ever-popular Sunday sermon topic. Sin, or missing the mark, is inevitable where there is free will. If we were incapable of sin, we would be robots. The first important thing about sin is to learn from our mistakes and not use them as an excuse to give up. The truth is that we learn far more from our mistakes than we do from our successes. A torpedo reaches its destination by making a series of mistakes and correcting them, but the torpedo doesn't get bawled out or bawl itself out for its errors!

The second important thing about sin is that we learn not to label ourselves or others as *sinners*. That tends to be a self-fulfilling prophecy. It's far more constructive to view ourselves as saints, which people apparently did in the early days of Christianity. We recall the old story of the little boy sitting in catechism class, looking up at the stained-glass windows and saying, "A saint is someone who lets the light through." Not a bad definition. Saints don't have to be sinless; they just have to keep realigning themselves with God. In the words of the old children's hymn,

> You can meet them in school, or in lanes, or at sea,
> In church, or in trains, or in shops, or at tea,
> For the saints of God are just folk like me,
> And I mean to be one too.

We weren't born missing the mark. One of the dumber things our society does is to condemn an innocent, helpless infant for whatever his parents may or may not have done. We were, however, born with a propensity to screw up. The more we remain aligned with God and God's perfect tailor-made possibilities for each occasion, the less we act on that propensity.

Chapter Five

Process theologians have dealt at length with the topic of vicarious atonement, the idea that Jesus somehow took the rap for our sins, once and for all. Few people in traditional Christianity seem to have paused to consider the illogicality of forgiveness for sins not yet committed by people not yet born. *Atonement* is often read *at-one-ment*, the idea of our getting back together with a God from whom we had become estranged. But we can never be separated from God except by deliberately shutting God out of our consciousness, and even then we can't entirely escape God's influence, so to atone is simply to stop doing that. We don't need a crucified savior for that. The great value of Jesus's death and resurrection is to show us what is possible, to show us love so deep, so broad, so high that it could forgive the people nailing him to the cross; coupled with a disciplined, God-centered mind that could even triumph over the death of the body, and return to demonstrate it. Certainly Jesus was at one with God. As Methodist minister Leslie Weatherhead has pointed out, Jesus, even while dying in agony on the cross, called God *Father*. He kept his attention focused on God and related to God as a person. Certainly under such conditions this was no mere nice metaphor; it was the core of Jesus's beliefs. A human being with human weaknesses and temptations, he lived his faith and remained unified with God to the end, showing us what is possible. If you want to call that atonement, go right ahead. As Eugene Peters, in his book *The Creative Advance*, puts it, "For the process theologian, the doctrine of divine love, sublimely symbolized in the life of Jesus, is the center about which all other considerations revolve. Insofar, process theism stands squarely within Christian faith."

In process terms, Jesus helped raise the overall level of the world by the quality of his life, an influence that still is felt by everyone and everything in some degree, even as the positive and negative qualities of our lives—less dramatically, perhaps—influence everything forever.

What To Do When the Roof Falls In

In challenging times, there are two things to keep in mind. *First*, align your mind with the mind of God for support and guidance. *Second*, when you need a helping hand, look first at the end of your arm.

True, there are times when there is virtually nothing you can do about a situation. That is when to "let go and let God," keeping your mind fixed on the outcome you want, rather than on a negative outcome. But such times are much rarer than we think. All too often, we have fallen into a pattern of dependency because of a child's view of life and of God. We wait for a miracle, for some adult or some kind of magic to rescue us, instead of seeing the wonder in all of life, because God is present in all of life. Mesle explains it well:

Morally, we can picture a divine love so great that in all events in every moment God is doing everything within God's power to bring about good, eagerly calling for the cooperation of all who will respond. But God works with a world in which agency is both fundamental and irrevocable, so that God cannot force the world's decisions. Scientifically, we can see here a God acting in *everything*, so that there are no *isolated* events that are "acts of God" standing outside the course of nature. The crucial vision here is of divine power as always present and active, but as always, inescapably woven with the causal forces of the world.

In this vision, God wishes and works to heal every diseased cell, to draw us away from every hateful thought. But neither the world nor we can be coerced by God. So we, with God, can rightfully celebrate when prayer and intelligence and good fortune combine to make the world more responsive to God's call. But even when the worst happens we can affirm that God is present with us, grieving with us, and working with us to create whatever good is possible out of the genuine evil we confront.

Grief

If you have suffered a great loss, there is the work of grieving to be done. However, the amount of time that grieving takes varies greatly with the individual. If you can let go of the belief that only by long and deep grieving do you show real caring, you can shorten your period of grief and get on with living a life that reflects positively on the person you have lost. Some people have used NLP techniques that allow one to regulate one's beliefs in order to shorten their deep grief period to a single morning; most of us probably wouldn't want to go quite that far. In any event, the length of one's grieving process has nothing to do with the depth of one's love for the person who has gone on. There are some cultures that regard death as a joyful occasion because the person who has died is free of earthly suffering; hence, there is little cause to grieve except for one's own sense of separation and loss.

Illness

If you are suffering an illness, the most effective prayer is "Thy will be done." God's will is always for your highest good. It is usually in your best interest to recover, and you usually do. Any physician can tell you that most illnesses are self-limiting. As we said in chapter four, if you are doing or failing to do something to your body in violation of natural law, stop! Feed and rest your body intelligently. Use herbs or other remedies judiciously. Keep picturing health and the activities you would like to pursue, and do not dwell on your misery any more than you can help. Since much illness is linked to failure to forgive, spend some of your quiet time in forgiving anyone who could possibly need your forgiveness, including yourself! (Remember that forgiveness is for the sake of getting the junk out of *your* consciousness, not for the sake of the other person.) Don't make things worse by smoking, or by excesses in eating or drinking, or by abuse of drugs. Be good to your body, and praise it for doing as well as it is doing. It's your means of learning and experiencing joys as well as sorrows in this lifetime.

Make sure that you are paying careful attention to the messages your body is sending you through pain and illness. Some people are better than others at noticing what is going on with their bodies. One thing for sure about any illness, minor or serious, is that it is trying to get your attention for some reason. If you take steps to remedy an illness while it is still minor or subtle, you can ward off a lot of difficulty.

Financial Challenges

If you are experiencing a financial challenge, the solution again begins in your mind, with your focusing on God as your source, not the job or the inheritance or the client. This is an abundant universe, and it is a well-established psychological fact that if you are mentally programmed for abundance, you will begin to see it all around you. Remember the story of the prophet Elisha and the widow in II Kings 4, when the creditor was coming to take her two sons to be slaves. Elisha asked her, "Tell me, what do you have in the house?" She had nothing but a jar of oil. Elisha told her to borrow as many empty containers as possible from the neighbors, to close the door, and to pour the oil she had into those containers. When they were all full, the oil ceased, she sold the containers, and paid her debt in full, with money left over for her and her sons to live on.

Your house symbolizes your mental state. As Unity minister Eric Butterworth explains in his book, *Spiritual Economics,*

> What [Elisha] was asking her was, "Where is your consciousness? What are you thinking about? What are you identifying with?" Her reply indicated that, despite the one pot of oil, she was centered in the awareness of poverty. She was possessed by fear, and thus had cut herself off from the divine flow. She had a pot of oil, but to her it was *only* one pot. It was evidence of substance, but to her it was a symbol of lack. She was plagued with the very common problem of "onliness."

Telling her to borrow the additional vessels suggests the need to expand the mind to include new faith and vision, to try on some new insights for size. She did borrow additional vessels, which meant she broadened her horizon of expectations. She poured the oil from her one pot into the new vessels, and it flowed freely till the last vessel was filled. When there were no more vessels, the oil stopped. In other words, as much as she could conceive and believe, she could achieve.

So if we are facing financial difficulties, we need to borrow additional vessels, raise our consciousness, widen our horizon of faith. "Identify yourself with the idea that you are entitled to the boundless support of the Universe," says Butterworth. But "the demand must be made before the supply can come forth to fill it. In other words, we must provide the vessels in which the oil may be increased." Jesus said that we must ask in order to receive. Butterworth points out that "the word 'ask' as Jesus uses it comes from the Greek root which has a strong connotation toward 'claim or demand'. We claim our good by creating the consciousness for it, by "building the house," as it says in Malachi.

That is the most outrageous feature of New Thought: right when things look darkest, we are expected to come up with the mental equivalent of a sunny day. Because that's the way the world works. Try it. If you want a sunny day, you have to create the mental equivalent of one first, no matter what the weather is outside. Remember, however, that you have to take appropriate action as well as think appropriate thoughts.

Relationship Difficulties

If you are having difficulties in a relationship, the challenge is to see God, or the Christ mind, in the other person. You are looking for the shift in your own perception that Marianne Williamson and *A Course In Miracles* call a miracle. This does not automatically make you wrong, or make you the one who necessarily has to change, except in consciousness. Whether you are wrong or being wronged, the solution is still to practice the presence of God.

Catherine Ponder tells the story of a woman who took literally the idea of seeing Christ in the other person and began picturing Jesus physically standing next to her husband all the time. This technique not only saved the marriage; it turned a sow's ear of a husband into a silk purse.

When we have a relationship difficulty, we usually think that things would be fine if only the other person would change. It never works. It can't. The only behavior you can control is your own. You can pray for another person's highest good, but you can't be sure that you know what it is, so you can't get too specific (that's called *outlining*). Therefore, it is *your* consciousness that has to change. You are part of the other person's environment, at least to some extent; and therefore, if you change, the person's environment is different. Changing any part of a system affects the rest of the system, and we are all parts of the same system. In process terms, we are all part of the pattern of the past.

If you find yourself starting to pout because you seem to be the one that has to do all the changing, ponder this principle from systems theory: In any system, all else being equal, the organism (that's you and us) with the greatest range of variables (that's flexibility) will dominate the system (comes out on top). True power is the ability to get along with the widest variety of people.

And remember Covey's Habits Four, Five, and Six: Think win-win, seek first to understand, and synergize. What would constitute a win for the problem boss, child, or spouse? How can you contribute to it in a way that constitutes a win for you, too? Takes ingenuity, and you have it.

Whatever the challenge, the solution is always you plus God within you. And it is true that "when the student is ready, the teacher will appear." When your mind is receptive, God is able to attract the perfect person, book, or other resource to you with exquisite timing. Stories abound of people who have found the much-needed screwdriver or roll of Scotch tape in the driveway (!), or the mechanic who showed up just in time to fix the car stranded in a remote location, or the ship that inexplicably changed course and went hundreds of miles out of its way so that it crossed the exact spot in the ocean where a sailor had fallen overboard in the middle of the night, unnoticed by his shipmates. The sailor's name was Bill Toles, and he had done what he could for himself by making a life preserver out of his dungarees and by not drinking the salt water, which would have killed him. Over and over he prayed, "Dear God, please let me be rescued," picturing both God and rescue. God takes care of the *how*; you just have to concentrate on the *what*.

The Black Hole

Feelings, Who-o-oa Feelings

No black hole chapter would be complete without a discussion of negative emotions such as blame, shame, guilt, fear, anxiety, anger, and any other rotten state of mind. They don't feel good. Some of us do our darndest to ignore them; others wallow in them, trapped, until they somehow dissipate. Neither approach works well.

Psychiatrist William Glasser likens feelings to the lights on the dashboard of your car. You don't drive down the road with your eyes glued on them, but you ignore them at your peril. Emotions are messengers from your subconscious mind. It is very important for you to notice them and what they are telling you. They sometimes masquerade as each other; for example, anger can be fear in disguise. Give your attention to the fact that you are angry as part of your current reality, and as you notice your anger, you may realize that it is covering up a fear of some sort, a defense against that fear. Some people say that all negative emotions are really fear. The antidote for fear is love: "Perfect love casteth out fear" (1 John 4:18). So you displace fear by putting your attention on God's unconditional love for you. That love guides and protects you in any circumstances. Emmet Fox's famous Golden Key technique is simply to stop thinking about the problem, whatever it is, and start reminding yourself of whatever you know about God. Think about God instead of thinking about the problem, about God's being present where the problem seems to be, and since your mind cannot entertain two thoughts at once, the negative emotions will vanish.

One of our favorite affirmations to use at difficult times is from Florence Scovel Shinn, author of the book *The Game of Life and How to Play It*: "I cast my burden on the Christ within, and I go free." Keep repeating it until you feel a shift in consciousness. "The Christ within" is God's initial aim, the mind of Christ that Jesus contacted and used better than anyone else before or since. By casting the burden, you are letting go of the pattern of the past and accepting more of God's perfect possibilities for you. The phrase, of course, comes from the Bible: "Cast thy burden upon the Lord, and he shall sustain thee (Ps. 55:22).

What about cynicism, or a just plain rotten personality? Both of these are habitual states of consciousness. The cure for both is the same as all the rest: to stop thinking about problems and start thinking about God, particularly about God as seen in other people and things. This is true whether you are the cynic or the person with the rotten personality, or have to put up with one.

Toxicity and Cults

Black holes can get even blacker and deeper if they involve a toxic religion. Much has already been written about toxic faiths, by Leo Booth and others. Any faith is toxic if it prevents you from living up to your full potential or keeps you living in fear. The God of unconditional love does not send punishment or retribution of any sort; only the consequences of violating the laws of a neutral universe do that, and they do it evenhandedly.

Much toxicity comes from belonging to a cult. The word *cult* used to mean a new offshoot of an established religion, and was a value-neutral word. Christianity began as a cult of Judaism. Lately, however, *cult* has come to have negative overtones, to the point that scholars have stopped using the word altogether. An organization is a cult, and therefore toxic, if:

1. it is authoritarian, demanding unquestioning obedience to an authority figure.

2. it discourages or forbids thinking for oneself.
3. it isolates one from the rest of one's family and friends, demanding that one give up one's personal assets.

Such tactics are frequently defended by a distorted or literal interpretation of Scripture.

People sometimes ask whether New Thought or one of its name-brand branches is a cult. New Thought "affirms the freedom of each individual in matters of belief," as it states in the International New Thought Alliance Declaration of Principles. It encourages people to think for themselves, and teaches people to get along better than ever with family and friends. It makes no demands on personal assets, although it does teach the ancient Biblical practice of tithing, giving the first tenth of one's income to God's work or workers, as a mental discipline for prosperity. But tithing is never compulsory, and must be done in the proper frame of mind to be effective.

Grownup or Adult?

Adults, having more experience, more freedom, and more physical strength and dexterity, have more problem-solving ability than children do. But what is an adult? The husband-and-wife team of Fran and Louis Cox address this question in their book, *A Conscious Life: Cultivating the Seven Qualities of Authentic Adulthood*. They comment,

> Useful definitions about what constitutes an adult are rare. Cheryl Merser, in her book *Grownups: A Generation in Search of Adulthood*, notes that in p.reindustrial Western culture there was no such official stage of life. "You were a man or a woman if you weren't a child, that's all, and the difference for men was

one of size, age, and physical capacity; girls became women when they became fertile."

The Coxes finally determined,

> *Adulthood is an internal affair, a state of mind, whereas being a grownup has to do with performing a given set of behaviors.* When we define adulthood by behaviors, we get caught in creating fixed forms. . . . Such a model is doomed by its inflexibility—and flexibility is a must for psychological health in times of rapid change. . . . Being grown up, as it is understood in this country, is not true adulthood, but rather a child's view of adulthood.

The Coxes outline a list of twelve beliefs, childish-sounding because they are formed in childhood, that represent being a grownup (not an adult). "Operating out of these beliefs inevitably leads to a sense of disappointment and unhappiness":

1. Your facades (personality, status, income, deeds) represent who you really are.
2. What you plan to have happen must happen exactly as planned if it is to have value.
3. You should be able to produce what you say you want immediately.
4. How you see reality is how it is.
5. When you get what you really want, you'll be satisfied.
6. You don't need to pay attention to your harmful behaviors, even when they keep repeating themselves.
7. Life should be easy because you deserve to be treated well.
8. Nothing can hurt you unless you let it.
9. You don't have to listen to your body.
10. You are in control of your mind.

11. If you behave in the right ways, you will be spared pain.
12. You can grow up to be somebody other than who you are.

As the Coxes observe,

> If these twelve beliefs represented reality—and many people, consciously or unconsciously, wish they did— you would never have to learn new things as a adult, make mistakes, make reparation, work hard, be creative, get to know your interior world, or really consider others.

It is easy to see how people with such beliefs could misinterpret New Thought principles, for example, trying to control their own minds (which we can never do completely because so much is unconscious) instead of aligning their minds with God and centering on God-given universal principles.

From these beliefs come the seven operating principles of the grownup:

1. I must control, dismiss, or merge with you.
2. Appearing vulnerable or flawed must always be avoided.
3. I pay attention only to "reality."
4. I must control my emotions at all times.
5. I must manage the moment and not let it surprise me.
6. I have power only when I control, dominate, or win.
7. My limits are either my fault, your fault, or God's fault.

In contrast, here are the seven operating principles of the adult:

1. I am here, and you are over there.
2. I am safe and sound inside my own skin.

3. I am curious about everything that goes on inside me.
4. I learn from my emotions.
5. I know there is nothing but now.
6. I always have power.
7. I always have limits.

These external realities, the Coxes explain, color behavior, but are not the same thing as behavior. Instead, they are the ground from which behavior emerges. The adult understands the need for lifelong learning, and that perfection is an illusion. Yet the adult self cannot just try to deny or wipe out the grownup self. Rather, "the adult self grows by expanding contact with the grownup self . . . grows in compassion and wisdom by paying attention and being loving to the wounded part of [it]."

Process theologian Marjorie Suchocki adds,

> Our trust must not be placed in our past ways, not even when those ways were enacted in response to concrete divine guidance. This would be akin to a person at age forty claiming that seven-year-old behavior was still appropriate, since once it had been in response to God's guidance. Our trust must be placed in God, who leads us in faithfulness into the future, and hence toward continued creative response to God's reign.

The Coxes cite Robert Fritz, author of *The Path of Least Resistance*, on the subject of creative energy. His research shows that most of us "are raised to hold one or both of two disempowering, unconscious beliefs. The first is *I am powerless to create what I want*; the second is *I don't deserve to have what I want*."

New Thought, especially Process New Thought, stands in direct opposition to those negative beliefs. All creation is cocreation with a loving God, and you can have whatever you can develop the consciousness for. If you can develop the consciousness for it, you deserve to have it.

It isn't easy, though. Deb wrote, in a response to a friend who had written, "This growing up really is a pain in the you-know where!":

> I really resonate to your statement, as I have been wrestling with this growing-up business for some little time lately. What's weird is that I thought I had already grown up long ago. Now I understand, from reading various books, notably Leo Booth's *The God Game: It's Your Move*, that I have a long way to go. Leo explains that the very language used in churches—and even in New Thought—is inclined to keep us childish in our understanding of and relationship to God. Learning that we are expected to hold up our end of the log in this cocreation business is quite a jolt. I also found a lot of magical thinking lurking in my subconscious, despite my seeing myself as the thoroughly grown up and responsible scientist.
>
> Such realizations leave one with that frightened feeling, "They have taken away my Lord and I know not where they have laid him." I can't just sit around like a good child and wait for God to make miracles; I have to do my part, whatever is available for me to do. Ouch. Here the process thought that Alan and I teach has helped me a lot, because it provides a working model of cocreation: God offers perfect possibilities tailor-made for each moment, and we are free to choose how much of those possibilities we are ready to accept and how much of the past to retain. God never forces us, but always lures us on toward greater good, the highest good

for all, the highest standard. If we go against universal laws, the laws just do their thing and we take the consequences. That's all there is to karma. Once we "get it," we are free to soar, because we understand that we are in charge of the soaring.

As a song from one of the Christmas cartoon specials goes, "Even a miracle needs a hand."

In Parting

One of our favorite sources for daily doses of spiritual vitamins is Richard Carlson's little book, *Don't Sweat the Small Stuff...And It's All Small Stuff.* The quickest way out of the black hole is to get things in proportion. You will always have a role to play in God's universe somewhere, somehow, forever, and as Robert Schuller says, "God will have the last word—and it will be good." It is all small stuff, when you look at it that way. Meanwhile, we are here to love and to learn, and Carlson has some great ideas for doing both.

The trick is to get past the mere intellectual agreement, "That makes sense"; or emotional resonance, "That feels right"; and integrate these suggestions into your very being. We know this is rather screwed-up anatomy, but head and heart somehow meet in the gut, the intuition, that blends and utilizes both. "Wisdom is a marriage—a synergy—of heart and mind," writes Stephen Covey.

Blending head and heart when you're used to operating solely in one or the other is going to feel weird at first, because it represents change, and as Deb likes to say, change is strange. It feels really strange to deliberately think yourself out of a bad mood, or play down the what-if fear thoughts in favor of what-if possibilities. However, if the outcome of a situation is uncertain, you have the power to influence it, just like the famous quantum physics example of Schroedinger's cat. The hypothetical cat is in a box rigged with some sort of poison pill, and the question is whether the cat is dead or alive. Your belief makes the difference. If you think the cat is dead, or if you think the cat is alive, you are right.

As we mentioned earlier, New Thought is often confused with New Age. New Age is made up of people who are genuinely seeking for better answers to the problems of life, genuinely seeking for a spiritual path. New Thoughters know where the path is, because they are already on it, even if they fall off once in a while. New Thoughters know enough to keep an open mind, but not to "dabble in the occult," which Charles Fillmore warned against. Without abandoning their Western roots and rationality, they learn from Eastern ideas and practices, especially the ones about centered attention and balance. As Joan Cline-McCrary puts it in her book about Divine Science founder Malinda Cramer, *Malinda Cramer's Hidden* Harmony,

> The gospel (good news) of the "new order" was not an attempt to replace Christianity but to heighten the understanding of those who called themselves Christians by adding (more correctly restoring) Eastern understanding to that of the West—one might say, by restoring the *heart* of the East to the *mind* of the West.

Above all, New Thoughters stay clearly aligned with God, following in the footsteps of Jesus, our elder brother and way-shower. New Thought can therefore be the heart and soul of a new age, can steer the world into "harmony and understanding," "when peace will guide the planets, and love will steer the stars."

Chapter Five

Bibliography

Anderson, C. Alan. *A Guide to the Selection and Care of Your Personal God.* Canton, Mass.: Squantum Press, 1991.

Anderson, C. Alan, and Deborah G. Whitehouse. *New Thought: A Practical American Spirituality.* New York: Crossroad Publishing Company, 1995.

Andreas, Steve, and Connirae Andreas. *Change Your Mind and Keep the Change.* Moab, Utah: Real People Press, 1987.

Anthony, Robert. "How to Have Everything You Want" audiotape. Scottsdale, Ariz.: Robert Anthony, no date.

Atkins, Robert. *Dr. Atkins' New Diet Revolution.* New York: Avon, 1992.

Batmanghelidj, F. *Your Body's Many Cries for Water.* Falls Church, Va.: Global Health Solutions, 1997.

Benson, Herbert. *Beyond the Relaxation Response.* New York: Berkley Books, 1985.

Booth, Leo. *The God Game: It's Your Move.* Walpole, N.H.: Stillpoint Publishing, 1994.

Bristol, Claude M., and Harold Sherman. *TNT: It Rocks the Earth.* Englewood Cliffs, N.J.: Prentice-Hall, 1954.

Butterworth, Eric. *Spiritual Economics.* Unity Village, Mo.: Unity Press, 1983.

Cady, H. Emilie. *Lessons in Truth.* Unity Village, Mo.: Unity Books, n.d.

Bibliography

Carlson, Richard. *Don't Sweat the Small Stuff...And It's All Small Stuff.* New York: Hyperion, 1997.

Cates, David. *Unconditional Money.* Willamina, Ore.: Buffalo Press, 1995.

Cline-McCrary (ed.). *Malinda Cramer's Hidden Harmony.* Denver: Divine Science Federation International, 1990.

Cobb, John B., Jr., and David Ray Griffin. *Process Theology: An Expository Introduction.* Philadelphia: The Westminster Press, 1976.

Covey, Stephen R. *The Seven Habits of Highly Effective People.* New York: Simon and Schuster, 1989.

Covey, Stephen R., A Roger Merrill, and Rebecca R. Merrill. *First Things First.* New York: Simon and Schuster, 1994.

Cox, Fran and Louis. *A Conscious Life: Cultivating the Seven Qualities of Authentic Adulthood.* Berkeley, Calif.: Conari Press, 1996.

Dalai Lama. *The Good Heart: A Buddhist Perspective on the Teachings of Jesus.* Wisdom Publications, 1996.

Diamond, Marilyn, and Dr. Donald Burton Schnell. *Fitonics for Life.* New York: Avon Books, 1996.

Dilts, Robert, Tim Hallbom, and Suzi Smith. *Beliefs: Pathways to Health and Well-Being.* Portland, Ore.: Metamorphous Press, 1990.

Dresser, Horatio W., ed. *The Spirit of the New Thought.* New York: Thomas Y. Crowell Company, 1917.

Bibliography

The Encyclopedia of Philosophy. New York and London: The Macmillan Company and The Free Press and Collier - Macmillan Limited, 1967.

Fisher, Mark. *The Instant Millionaire*. San Rafael, Calif.: New World Library, 1990.

Ford, Edward. "An Overwhelmed Single Parent". In Glasser, Naomi (Ed.). *What Are You Doing? How People Are Helped Through Reality Therapy*. New York: Harper and Row, 1980.

Fox, Emmet. *Alter Your Life*. New York: Harper and Brothers, 1950.

------ *Diagrams for Living*. New York: Harper and Row, 1968.

------ *Make Your Life Worth While*. New York: Harper and Brothers, 1942.

------ *The Sermon On the Mount*. New York: Harper and Row, 1938.

Fritz, Robert. *The Path of Least Resistance*. New York: Fawcett Columbine, 1989.

Gittleman, Ann Louise. *Your Body Knows Best*. New York: Pocket Books, 1997.

Glasser, William. *Positive Addiction*. New York: HarperCollins, 1985.

Gray, John. *Men Are From Mars, Women Are From Venus*. New York: HarperCollins, 1992.

Bibliography

Griffin, David Ray. *God, Power, and Evil: A Process Theodicy.* Philadephia: The Westminster Press, 1976.

Griffin, David Ray, and Huston Smith. *Primordial Truth and Postmodern Theology.* Albany: State University of New York Press, 1989.

Hartshorne, Charles. *Omnipotence and Other Theological Mistakes.* Albany: State University of New York, 1984.

------ *The Philosophy of Charles Hartshorne.* (Ed. Lewis Edwin Hahn). La Salle, Ill.: Open Court, 1991.

Huber, Richard M. *The American Way of Success.* New York: McGraw-Hill, 1971.

Inge, William Ralph. *Personal Idealism and Mysticism.* London: Longmans, Green and Co., 1913.

------ *Outspoken Essays.* Second series. London: Longmans, Green and Co., 1923.

Kaufman, Barry Neil. *Happiness is a Choice.* New York: Fawcett-Columbine, 1991.

------ *To Love is To Be Happy With.* New York: Fawcett Crest, 1977.

Laut, Phil. *Money is Your Friend.* New York: Ivy Books, 1989.

Lawrence, Brother. *The Practice of the Presence of God.* Translated by John J. Delaney. New York: Image (Doubleday), 1977.

Bibliography

Leonard, George. *Mastery: The Keys to Success and Long-Term Fulfillment.* New York: Plume (Penguin Group), 1992.

MacFague, Sallie. *Models of God: Theology For an Ecological,Nuclear Age.* Philadelphia: Fortress Press, 1987.

Marshall, Catherine. *A Man Called Peter.* New York: Avon Books, 1994.

Merser, Cheryl. *Grownups: A Generation in Search of Adulthood.* New York: Penguin, 1990.

Mesle, Robert C. *Process Theology: A Basic Introduction.* St Louis, Mo.: Chalice Press, 1993.

Morrissey, Mary. *Building Your Field of Dreams.* New York: Simon & Schuster, 1996.

Peters, Eugene H. *The Creative Advance.* St. Louis, Mo.: The Bethany Press, 1966.

Pilzer, Paul. *God Wants You to Be Rich: The Theory of Economics.* New York: Simon & Schuster, 1995.

Ponder, Catherine. *The Dynamic Laws of Prosperity.* Englewood Cliffs, N.J.: Prentice-Hall, 1962.

------ *The Dynamic Laws of Healing.* Marina del Rey, Calif.: DeVorss, 1985.

------ *The Prospering Power of Love.* Unity Village, Mo.: Unity Press, 1966.

------ *The Prosperity Secret of the Ages.* Englewood Cliffs, N.J.: Prentice-Hall, 1964.

Bibliography

Rosemergy, Jim. *Even Mystics Have Bills to Pay.* Lee's Summit, Mo.: Inner Journey, 1994.

Senge, Peter. *The Fifth Discipline.* New York: Currency/Doubleday, 1990.

Sher, Barbara. *Wishcraft.* New York: Ballantine, 1979.

------ *Live the Life You Love in Ten Step-By-Step Lessons.* New York: Delacorte, 1996.

------ *Teamswork!.* New York: Warner Books, 1989.

Shinn, Florence Scovel. *The Wisdom of Florence Scovel Shinn: 4 Complete Books.* New York: Fireside, 1989.

Silva, José, and Robert B. Stone. *You, the Healer.* Tiburon, Calif.: H. J. Kramer, Inc., 1989.

Snowden, James H. *The Truth About Christian Science.* Philadelphia: The Westminster Press, 1920.

Suchocki, Marjorie Hewitt. *God Christ Church: A Practical Guide to Process Theology*, New revised edition. New York: Crossroad Publishing Company, 1995.

Thiede, Carsten Peter, and Matthew D'Ancona. *Eyewitness to Jesus.* New York: Doubleday, 1996.

Wattles, Wallace. *Financial Success Through Creative Mind Power.* (Originally titled *The Science of Getting Rich*). Glendale, Calif.: Westwood Publishing Company, 1986.

Bibliography

Weatherhead, Leslie. *The Christian Agnostic*. Nashville, Tenn.: Abingdon Press, 1965.

Whitehead, Alfred North. *Process and Reality*. New York: The Macmillan Company, 1929.

Weil, Andrew. *Health and Healing*. Boston: Houghton-Mifflin, 1983.

Wilber, Ken. *Eye to Eye: The Quest for the New Paradigm*, expanded edition. Boston and Shaftesbury: Shambala Publications, Inc., 1990.

Williamson, Marianne. *A Return to Love*. New York: HarperCollins, 1992.

Bibliography

ABOUT THE AUTHORS

Drs. Deb Whitehouse and Alan Anderson are a husband-and-wife team of educators, scholars who have studied the history of the century-old New Thought movement and practiced its teachings for many years. Both of them are currently members of the Executive Board of the International New Thought Alliance (INTA), and Deb is editor of the INTA magazine, *New Thought*. Both have spoken and written extensively about New Thought, collaborating on an earlier book, *New Thought: A Practical American Spirituality* (Crossroad, 1995).

Deb holds a doctorate in educational psychology from Northern Illinois University in addition to degrees in music from Northwestern University. Alan's doctorate from Boston University is in philosophy; his doctoral dissertation is titled "Horatio W. Dresser and the Philosophy of New Thought," later published as *Healing Hypotheses* . He was part of a team of editors assisting Ervin Seale in publishing the complete works of the father of New Thought, *Phineas Parkhurst Quimby: The Complete Writings* (DeVorss). He also holds degrees in law, education, and political science. Alan is Professor of Philosophy and Religion (Emeritus) at Curry College in Milton, Massachusetts. The two of them have team-taught a course titled "Self Leadership Through Mind Management." Deb developed the course, which adds philosophical background in ethics and metaphysics to the work of Stephen Covey, author of the best-selling book, *The Seven Habits of Highly Effective People.* Covey's work is based largely on American success literature, which is in turn based largely on New Thought principles.

Alan was a pioneer in giving New Thought a presence on the World Wide Web, establishing the New Thought Movement Home Page in 1995. You can visit it at websyte.com/alan, where there are links to other New Thought materials and organizations. Alan and Deb's own web page is at http://neweverymoment.com.

Deb and Alan share a passion for Gilbert and Sullivan, for walks along the ocean, and for skewering sacred cows.

Printed in the United States
3292